# LETTERING &
# SIGN CARVING
## WORKBOOK

# LETTERING &
# SIGN CARVING
## WORKBOOK

### 10 SKILL-BUILDING PROJECTS FOR
### CARVING AND PAINTING CUSTOM SIGNS

Betty Padden

FOX CHAPEL
PUBLISHING

© 2011 by Fox Chapel Publishing Company, Inc. and Betty Padden.
All rights reserved.

*Lettering & Sign Carving Workbook* is an original work, first published in 2011
by Fox Chapel Publishing Company, Inc., East Petersburg, PA.
The patterns contained herein are copyrighted by the author. Readers may make
copies of these patterns for personal use. The patterns themselves, however, are not
to be duplicated for resale or distribution under any circumstances. Any such copying
is a violation of copyright law.

ISBN 978-1-56523-452-9

Library of Congress Cataloging-in-Publication Data


Padden, Betty.

Lettering & sign carving workbook / Betty Padden.

   p. cm.

Includes index.

ISBN 978-1-56523-452-9

1. Signs and signboards--Design and construction. 2. Wood-carving--Patterns. 3. Lettering. I.
Title. II. Title: Lettering and sign carving workbook.

TT360.P33 2011

736'.4--dc22

           2010038532

To learn more about the other great books from Fox Chapel Publishing, or to find a retailer near
you, call toll-free 800-457-9112 or visit us at *www.FoxChapelPublishing.com*.


**Note to Authors:** We are always looking for talented authors to write new books
in our area of woodworking, design, and related crafts. Please send a brief letter
describing your idea to Acquisition Editor, 1970 Broad Street, East Petersburg, PA 17520.


Printed in China
First Printing: January 2011

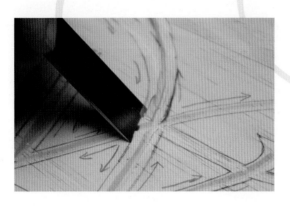

*To my husband, Bob, and my children, Joe, Tom, and Brianne,*
*for their love, support, and patience; and to my students,*
*for the joy they bring to my life.*

 Betty Padden has been making a living creating handsome wooden signs since 1976. With her husband, Bob, she owns Wooden Apple Signmakers. Their signs have been displayed at Walt Disney World, Disneyland, Busch Gardens, and other famous venues, as well as adorning businesses from Maine to Alaska. Betty and Bob have been teaching carving classes for 32 years at their studio. Betty also does design work for companies such as Ne Qwa Art and Blossom Bucket. Visit their website at *www.woodenapplesignmakers.com.*

# TABLE OF CONTENTS

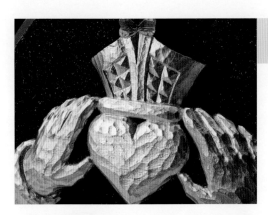

# CHAPTER 1

# CIRCA BOARD

A circa board is a small plaque decorated with the build date of a home or building. Although usually mounted on historic homes, there is currently a trend to put them on any home, no matter when the house was built. A circa board is a beautiful detail on your home, and it makes a nice, thoughtful gift for a housewarming. Though this project is specially designed to be easily accomplished by a novice carver, it is equally fun and useful for a more advanced carver.

Although many species of wood can be used for sign making, I am using white Eastern pine for this sign and most projects covered in this book. It is readily available at local lumberyards and even some of the big box stores. It's easy to carve and work with, and it's relatively inexpensive. With the proper finishes and upkeep, it also tends to weather well.

The design shape for this project is a simple rectangle, ¾" x 7¼" x 14" (20mm x 184mm x 356mm). For simplicity's sake, I have chosen a lumber dimension usually found in stock. Please note that when you look for it, it will be labeled 1" x 8" (25mm x 203mm) x a varying number of feet long, but will actually measure ¾" x 7¼" (19mm x 184mm). The size of board is called 1 x 8 because that was the original rough-cut size of the board before planing at the lumber mill. It is standard industry terminology. It pays to remember this when ordering wood for projects. Take care to choose the best grade or quality of lumber available, and check to see it is free of warping, checks and knots, and sap pockets.

## NEW TOPICS IN THIS CHAPTER

> The basics of laying out a sign

> Woodcarving chisels and their uses, care, and safety

> Basic letter carving and chip carving

> Beginner's painting techniques

## MATERIALS & TOOLS

- Sign blank, cut to ¾" x 7¼" x 14" (19mm x 184mm x 356mm)
- Full-size pattern of berries and leaves
- Number sheet
- Carbon paper
- Pencil
- Ruler (see-through grid ruler is ideal)
- Tape
- C-clamp and scrap wood
- Non-skid pad
- #13 6mm V-groove chisel
- #2 8mm chisel
- #2 16mm chisel (a #2 20 mm is also useful, but you can substitute the 16mm)
- #5 12mm chisel
- #5 16mm chisel (a #5 20mm is useful, but you can use the 16mm instead)
- #7 8mm chisel
- #7 14 mm chisel

A note about chisel sizes—whenever you run across a chisel size that you don't have, you can substitute a smaller mm size of the same sweep number.

**Carving Directions for Numbers**
Copy at 150%.

Arrows indicate starting points
Lines indicate stopping points
Scoop all rounded ends with a #11 7mm chisel

**Leaves and Berries**
Copy at 100%.

## LAYING OUT THE SIGN

**1 Mark the board.** Cut the board to 14" (356mm) long. Draw a line down the center from top to bottom. Next, measure 2⅞" (73mm) up from the bottom and draw a horizonal letter line. Draw a line ½" (13mm) in from the edge of the sign blank along all four edges. Draw a line on the sides ⅜" (10mm) down from the surface. Hold the pencil tip on the mark and put your ring finger on the surface. Slide your hand to mark the bottom of the bevel.

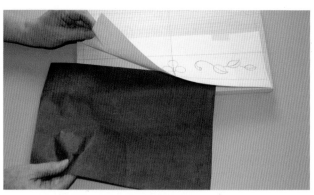

**2 Transfer the leaf and berry pattern.** Tape the top edge of the leaf and berry pattern to the blank. Line up the centerline of the pattern to the centerline and the letter line drawn on the blank. Slip the carbon paper under the pattern. Transfer the pattern.

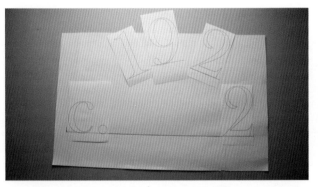

**3 Assemble the number pattern.** The numbers should measure 3½" (89mm) tall. Cut apart the numbers you need. Tape together two pieces of paper. On this paper, draw a line 2" (51mm) up from the bottom, 12" (305mm) long. Tape the "c." and numbers to the paper. Match up the lines under the numbers to the line on the paper. Tape the "c." first, and then the last number. Notice numbers with rounded bottoms fall below the line—if those characters aren't drawn slightly larger, they will appear too small when next to flat-bottomed characters.

**4 Space the numbers.** Correct spacing of lettering is done by eye. Look at the overall size of the area between the lettering, and try to balance that or maintain it throughout the word. After you are happy with the spacing, you need to find the center of the entire text field to place it on the blank. Measure to find the center of the circa date. Fold the paper at this point, taking care to fold a line perpendicular to the line under the numbers. Match the letter line on the sign to the line beneath the numbers, and the centerline on the sign blank to the center fold of the pattern. Tape along one side only, as before.

**5 Transfer the pattern.** Take a moment to thicken some of the thinner sections of the numbers and point the serifs—they are the points that extend out from the letter ends. Be consistent! If you increase a thin line by ⅛" (3mm), thicken all thin lines by the same amount.

**6 Add stopcut marks.** When the design is on the board and all corrections have been made, draw stop cuts down the center of the numbers and angled into the serifs. Your first chisel cuts will be on these lines. As you become more skilled, you won't need to do this.

# A BRIEF DISCUSSION ABOUT WOOD GRAIN

Understanding the structure of wood grain will make working with and controlling wood much easier, resulting in a cleaner, more professional-looking carving.

The best way to think about wood grain and understand how it will react to your chisel cuts is to picture a bundle of thin hollow tubes or straws bundled together.

The bonds holding the straws together are weak—they will easily split or fracture if a knife or chisel cut starts at the end of a straw. This property is useful in splitting firewood. The surface at the end of a block or log where all the straws end is called, appropriately enough, the end grain.

Below, you will see the wrong way to approach the wood grain. After some experience, reading the grain will become second nature to you. Until then, drawing guidelines on letters and numbers helps (see page 10).

Whenever the wood starts to fracture or split as you are carving, you are probably carving against the grain. Simply reversing the direction of your cut should stop the fracturing. In the rare event that this does not work, you can carve at right angles to the grain.

Closeup of straw-like structure of wood fibers.

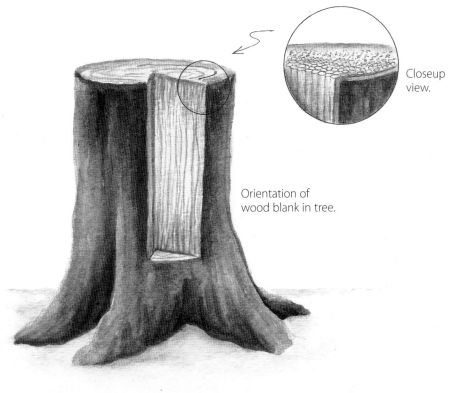

Closeup view.

Orientation of wood blank in tree.

Wrong direction— against the grain.

The straw-like wood fibers in the wood blank are not always straight or flat—they can slant up or down, so it is important to be able to read the grain direction.

When the cutting edge cuts into the ends of the wood fibers, they split readily and cause fracturing. Simply reversing direction will correct this.

## PRACTICE: CARVING THE NUMBER 1

If this is your first time carving letters, it's a good idea to practice on a scrap piece of pine. This way, any mistakes you may make while getting the hang of things won't ruin a good sign blank. Trace an assortment of numbers you will be using. Pick some that are straight, and some others that have rounded parts to them. "1," "2," and "9" would be good choices to use. Transfer a few of each of these numbers to a practice board. Be sure to add stop-cut lines to the numerals. You will need only the #2 16mm and a #13 6mm V-groove to carve this number.

**1** **Clamp the blank.** Secure the board with two clamps to the carving bench before starting to carve. I place a piece of non-skid pad (the kind used under rugs) under the board before securing it to the bench with two C-clamps. It is very important to securely clamp the board to the bench so both hands can remain on the chisel. Many injuries occur when novice carvers use one hand to hold the sign.

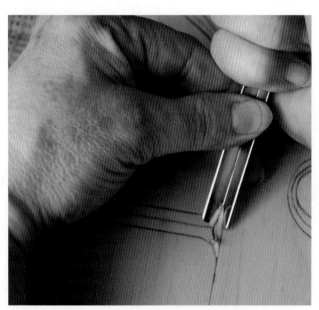

**2** **Cut serifs.** Cut the serifs first. Using the #13 6mm V-groove, begin on the bottom of the numeral. Start from the outer tip in a very shallow cut and push the V-groove into the center of the serif, cutting deeper as you go.

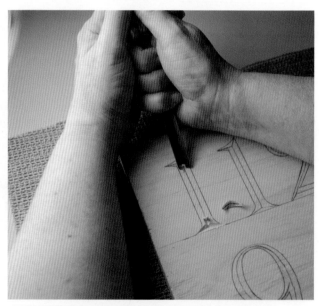

**3** **Stop-cut the centerline.** Begin stop-cutting the centerline of the 1. You can begin at the top or the bottom.

# Two grips

There are two ways to hold a chisel. The first way is to grip the metal part of the chisel fairly close to the edge, with your left hand if you are right-handed (right hand if you are left-handed). Grip the wooden handle with your other hand. This is how to hold the chisel when you want to carve away from yourself.

Sometimes it is necessary or more comfortable to carve by pulling the chisel toward you. Most people feel very insecure doing this, but if you grip the chisel on the metal portion as shown, you will have control of the cut. Be sure to anchor both forearms or wrists securely on the bench as shown at all times, and you will find it is nearly impossible to get the chisel edge close enough to cut you.

The first grip.

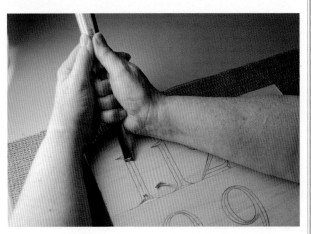

The second grip.

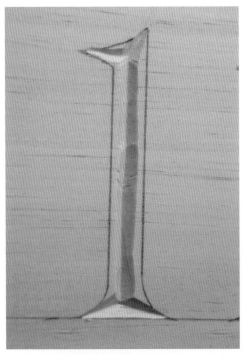

**TIP**

### Keeping Your Line Straight

Place half of the edge of the chisel on the line, leaving the other half on the portion of the previous cut. This will ensure you maintain the same angle when carving the number.

4 **Cut the top serifs.** Cut the top serifs in the same way you did the bottom serifs.

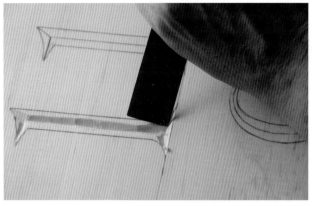

**5** **Slice the bottom serifs.** Using the corner of the #2 16mm chisel, begin slicing the wood in the serif so the cut angles from the drawn edge of the letter to the bottom of the stop cut.

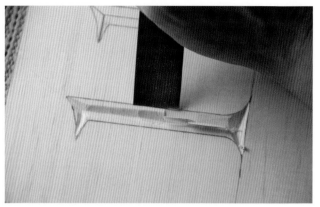

**6** **Begin carving the main body.** Set the edge of the chisel on or in front of the line. The remnants of the pencil line allow you to see if the carved line is straight. Carve the angle down into the stop cut by pushing the chisel at an angle—thereby slicing the cut.

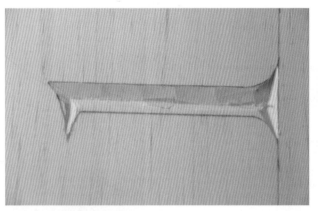

**7** **Cut the rest of the side.** Continue up the side of the 1 until you reach the curve of the serif.

**8** **Cut in the top serifs.** Now cut in the top serifs in the same way as the lower ones.

**9** **Cut the other side of the body.** Using the #2 chisel, carve the other side of the main body in the same manner as the first side.

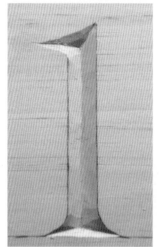

**10** **Clean the carving.** When the entire number has been carved, begin cleaning the carving so there are no stray splinters or chips left. Do this by gently pushing the #2 chisel into the center V trench at the bottom. Take care not to cut a deep gouge there. You've completed carving the number 1.

# PRACTICE: CARVING THE NUMBER 2

Wood grain really comes into play when carving a curved letter or number. It is useful to draw in directional lines (seen in the following steps) to show where the grain is. Get out the following chisels: #13 6mm V-groove, #2 8mm, # 2 16mm or 20mm, #5 16mm, and #7 14mm.

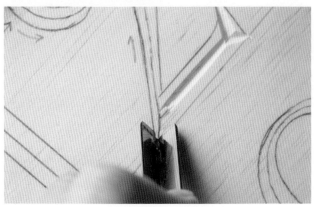

1 **Make bottom stop-cuts.** Draw grain guidelines. Note the arrow marks. These indicate where to begin each cut. Stop-cut the right-side serifs. Stop-cut the bottom line. Stop-cut the left-corner serif.

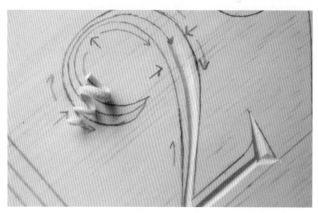

2 **Stop-cut the leg.** Begin stop-cutting the leg of the 2. Stop at the midpoint of the curve.

3 **Carve from the top.** Start at the highest point of the 2 and bring a stop-cut down to meet the previous cut.

4 **Complete the stop-cutting.** Start at the tip of the 2 and create a stop cut up to the midpoint of curve.

5 **Slice the bottom line of the foot.** Using the #2 20 mm chisel, begin the first slice up from the bottom line into the stop cut on the foot of the 2. Remember to overlap your cuts so the finished plane is at a consistent angle. Continue for the length of the line. Cut down from the top line of the foot to the bottom of the stop cut.

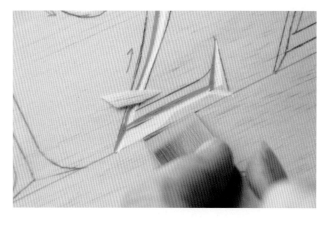

**Cut the curve.**

**Cut the straight side.**

6 **Cut in the bottom serif.** Cut in the curve of the bottom serif using the corner of the #2 chisel. Take lots of small cuts to get around the curve. Continue using the corner of the #2 chisel to cut in the straight side of the serif.

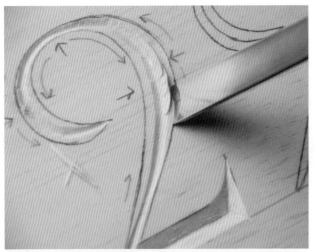

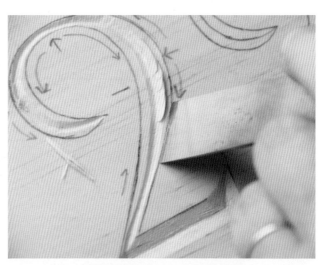

7 **Cut the outside right curve.** Using the #5 16mm chisel, carve the outside edge of the 2's right side, starting at the arrow and slicing down into the stop cut. Proceed downward. Notice part of the chisel is in the previously carved portion of the 2—this helps to maintain the same angle throughout. Continue using the #5 chisel while you cut the outside curve.

8 **Cut the straight part of the outside line.** Because the line is now pretty straight, switch chisels to a #2 16mm. Make chisel cuts down the leg of the 2 until you reach the foot. Notice how the narrower part of the leg is not as deep as the foot.

**TIP**

**Choosing a Chisel**

When trying to decide what chisel to use on a curve, match the shape of the curve to the curve of the chisel. Always choose a tool that is more curved rather than less curved. A smaller curve will fit into the larger curve, while a too-large chisel curve will destroy the shape you wanted in your carving.

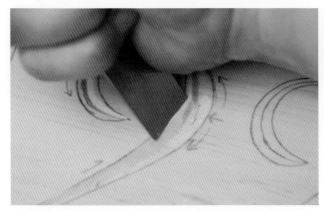

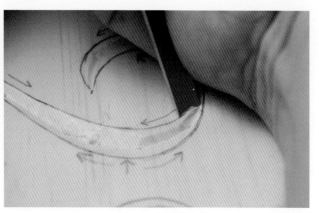

9 **Carve up the left side of the leg.** Start carving up the leg with a #2 16mm chisel in the direction of the arrows. Carve until you reach the start of the curve.

10 **Carve the left side of the curve.** Starting at the top left of the 2 inside the curve, use a #2 8mm chisel to carve in this area. Follow the arrow downward. Continue carving to meet up with the cut that came up the leg. Note the wood chips are still attached to the carving— they will be cut free when we do the cleaning stage.

11 **Carve up the outside line of the leg.** Switch to the #5 16 mm chisel again. Resume carving of the outer curve of the leg, traveling in the direction of the arrow. Switch to the second holding method for the last few cuts, where the line is almost flat. Stop when you reach the marker arrow—if you continue past this point, you will fracture the wood.

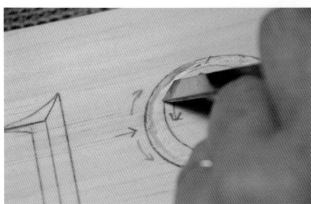

12 **Carve down the inside of the left curve.** Use the #2 8mm to carve the inside curve of the left side of the 2. Begin at the top and proceed downward until you reach the midpoint opposite the arrow.

13 **Carve up the inside of the left curve.** With the same #2 8mm chisel, start carving up the inside of the left curve. Begin at the top edge of the point. Carve up the curve to the midpoint. Finish by blending the two areas.

**14** **Carve the outer curve of the left side.**
Switch chisels to the #7 14mm, which will fit this tight curve. Start carving at the midpoint arrow on the outer curve of the left side of the 2. Proceed up the curve in the direction of the arrow. Continue slicing up to the top of the 2. Note that some of the wood chips remain attached to the base of the cut. These will be removed when we clean the number. Blend the last cuts into the previously carved edge.

**15** **Carve the lower portion of the outside left curve.** Carve the lower half of the curve, beginning at the midpoint marker arrow. Proceed to carve the edge downward. Make the last cut on the lower edge of the point.

**16** **Clean out the chips.** Using the #2 8mm chisel, begin cleaning the wood chips still attached to the carving by gently pushing the chisel down in the deepest point of the cut, taking care not to cut a trench in the base. If the chips still won't come free, you may need to cut from each angle a few times. Always use the same chisel you carved with to do this. You can also use the #13 V-groove. Be careful to skim across the bottom—don't cut into the carving.

# PRACTICE: CARVING THE NUMBER 9

The nine is similar to the number two in that both are curved numbers, and so, many of the techniques used are repeated. The main differences are the absence of the foot, and the curve of the top of the nine continues, forming a complete circle. The chisels you will need for this are the #13 6mm V-groove, the #2 8mm, the #5 12mm, the #5 16 or 20mm (I'm using a 20mm here), and the #11 7mm.

**1 Begin the stop-cutting.** Begin cutting the stop cuts with the #13 V-groove at the tail of the 9 to the bottom of the curve. Stop-cut downward from the midpoint of the leg.

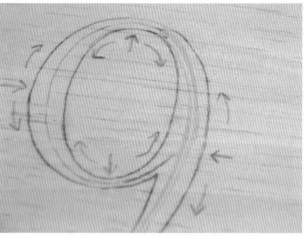

**2 Stop-cut upward from the midpoint of the leg.** Start from the midpoint of the right side and continue up to the top of the 9.

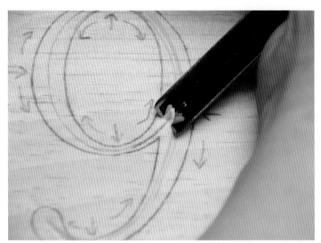

**3 Stop-cut the bottom of the loop.** Next, stop-cut the connector line at the middle of the right leg. Continue to the marker arrow on the bottom of the loop.

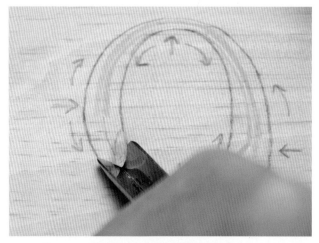

**4 Stop-cut the top and left of the loop.** Begin the next stop cut at the top of the 9. Follow the arrows marked on the inside of the loop. Continue the cut around and down to the midpoint of the left side. Then, cut up from the bottom until you hit the same midpoint. This completes the stop cuts on the 9.

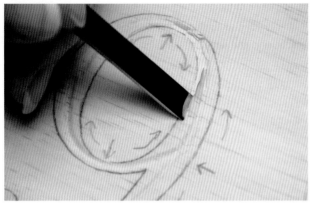

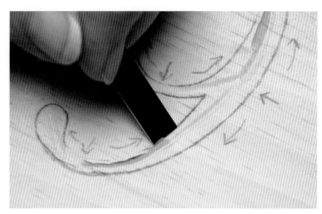

5 **Carve the inner upper curve.** Using the #2 8mm chisel, begin carving the inner curve of the 9 at the top of the loop. Continue carving the inner curve down to the right. Remember to keep some of the pencil line as you carve. Finish the cut at the center of the right curve.

6 **Carve the inner curve of the tail.** Move to the tail of the 9 and continue carving with the #2 8mm chisel. Cut the inner curve of the number. Bring the cut through the connector line, and join the two carved edges of the inner curve.

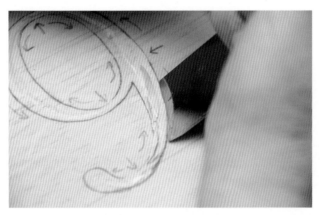

7 **Carve the outer right curve.** Using a #5 20mm chisel, begin carving the outer curve of the 9 on the right side at the arrow at the center. Carve down the side in the direction of the arrow. Stop when you reach the narrow part of the number.

8 **Carve the narrow part of the tail.** You've now reached a part of the number where the curve is tighter. Switch to a smaller #5 12mm chisel. Continue carving to the bottom of the tail and stop.

9 **Carve the outer upper right curve.** Switch to a #5 20mm chisel to carve the outer edge of the 9 from the midpoint to the top. Stop when you reach the narrow part of the number toward the top. As you approach the top, you will need to switch to a smaller #5 12mm chisel. Continue to the top of the 9 and stop at the midpoint arrow.

10 **Carve the inner upper curve.** Using a #2 8mm chisel, begin carving the inner upper curve. Start at the arrow at the bottom of the loop. Continue carving upward. Make the last cut at the midpoint of the curve, across from the arrow.

11 **Carve the inner left curve.** Move to the top of the inner curve of the loop and begin carving down to the left. Join the two carved edges at the center point.

12 **Carve the outer upper left curve.** Using the #5 20mm chisel, begin carving the outer curve of the left side of the 9, starting at the arrow at the midpoint. Continue carving up toward the top of the loop in the direction of the arrow. Stop at the top.

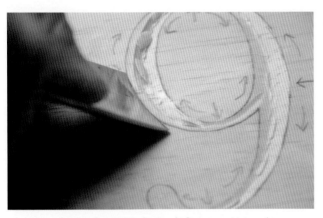

13 **Carve the outer lower left curve.** Using the same #5 20mm chisel, begin carving the lower quadrant of the outer curve of the loop. Start at the midpoint arrow and continue carving downward until you reach the narrow part of the number.

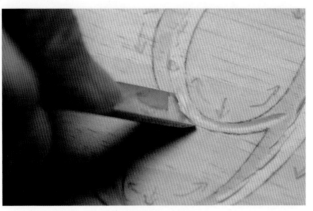

14 **Carve the bottom outside of the loop.** Switch to the smaller #5 12mm to carve the tighter curve at the bottom of the loop. Carve down from the left side to the center point, stop, and then carve down from the right to the center.

15 **Carve the tip of the tail.** Use the #11 7mm chisel to scoop out the center of the round tip on the tail. Using one side of the chisel, scoop out the lower edge in the direction shown (with the grain). Next, scoop out the right side of the rounded tip by carving upward. Blend the cuts.

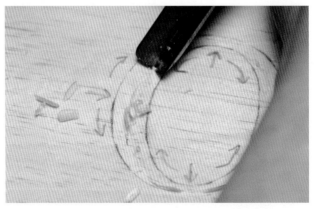

16 **Clean out the chips.** Clean the 9 using a #13 V-groove, as we did for the 2 (see page 20). You can also use the other methods discussed to clean out the 2.

## CARVING THE CIRCA BOARD AND NUMBERS

Once you feel confident in carving these numbers (repeating them as many times as you need to), you should be able to carve any number. Practice carving the numbers that you want on your final sign. When you're ready, move on to carving the circa board.

1 **Look over the layout.** Look over the layout you prepared for the sign and make sure everything is as you want it. Clamp the board. Use a scrap of wood under the C-clamp to prevent damage to the sign. Remember to put anti-skid material under the board.

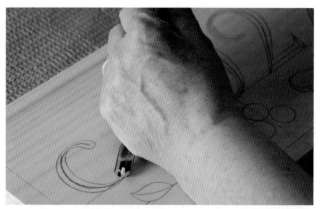

2 **Stop-cut the c.** Stop-cut the c using the #13 V-groove. Because carving the c is much the same as carving the 9, I will touch upon the process without going in depth.

3 **Carve half of the inside curve of the c.** Begin carving the inside curve of the c starting at the arrow (either top or bottom) and moving to the midpoint of the letter. Use a #2 8mm chisel. You can start on the top or the bottom. Here, I started on the bottom.

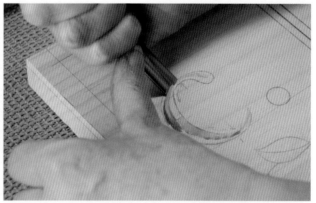

4 **Carve the outside curve of the c.** Carve the outside curve of the c using the #5 12mm gouge. Proceed to finish the rest of the c using the same techniques you used to carve the 9 (page 21). Scoop out the tip of the c. Clean out the chips.

> **NOTE**
>
> **Carve the Numbers**
> At this point, go on to carve the rest of the numbers in the sign. For instructional purposes, I will skip ahead and show you how to carve the leaves and berries. Refer back to the practice carving steps for the numbers 2 and 9 (page 17 and page 21) to answer any questions about curved numbers, and the step-by-step for the number 1 (page 14) to address questions on straight numbers.

**5** **Carve the beveled edge on the end-grain edges.** Use a #2 20mm chisel. Place the chisel edge just before the pencil line, with a small portion of the chisel not on the sign. Slice down toward the guideline. For the following cuts, place only part of the chisel on the uncut portion. Keeping some of the chisel on the previously cut edge allows you to maintain the angle. When finished with your preliminary pass, go back over the cuts to deepen the angle to the guideline.

**6** **Carve a bevel on the top and bottom.** Carving the bevel on the top and bottom requires a different technique because it is parallel to the wood grain. Start with a small slice at first to test for fracturing. If there isn't any, increase the length and depth of the cut, continuing in the same direction. If fracturing did occur, simply reverse the direction you are carving in.

**7** **Carve the corners of the border.** As you continue carving to the end of this side, your bevel will meet the previously carved bevel on the side. You will find that when these two bevels meet, a ridge will form, running at an angle from the top to the guideline.

## CHIP-CARVING THE LEAVES AND BERRIES

Chip carving, or incised carving, is a great way to add dimension to your project. The best way to understand it is to think of it as the reverse of relief, or raised, carving. It is a faster method of carving than relief carving, which makes it ideal for projects where time is an issue. You will be using the following chisels: #13 6mm V-groove, the #5 12mm, the #7 8mm, the #7 14mm (if you need to, you can substitute the #7 8mm), and the #11 7mm.

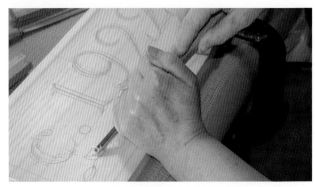

**1** **Stop-cut the center vein.** Stop-cut the center vein with the #13 V-groove. Start at the tip of the leaf with a very slight cut, and steadily increase the depth as you move to the center. Stop and repeat from the other end of the leaf.

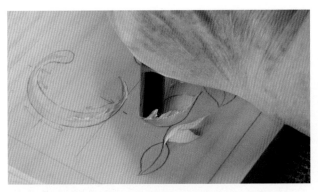

**2** **Carve the leaf.** Using the #5 12mm chisel, cut into the stop cut from the outer edge on one side. Continue toward the tip of the leaf. When done on one side, repeat on the other side, taking care to cut with the grain. When both sides are cut, tidy up any chips. Cut all the rest of the leaves.

**3** **Carve the berries.** Start scooping out the berry using a #7 14mm chisel. Position the chisel edge on the edge of the berry and make a very slight cut about half of the distance toward the center. Repeat around the edge of the berry until the center comes free. Finish carving the edge on the rest of the berry. Clean and smooth the berry. Carve the other berries.

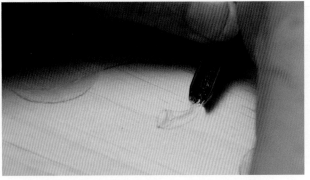

**4** **Stop-cut the center and end of the stem.** The only part of the stem that will be carved is the wide part—the areas that are only lines will be painted, not carved. Begin with a stop cut down the middle, using the #13 V-groove. Cut into the center of the stem from one corner. Repeat on the opposite side. Using a #11 7mm veiner, begin scooping inward at the end of the stem. Clean the sides of the stem.

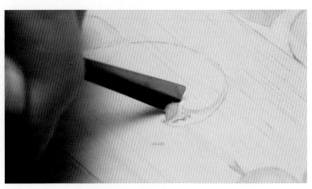

**5** **Cut the end of the stem.** Use a #7 8mm fishtail to cut the end of the stem down at an angle to meet the stop cut. Clean out any chips. Carve the other stems. You've now completed the carving of the sign.

# PREPARE THE SIGN FOR FINISHING

When a sign or carving is to be used outside, priming and painting it with latex finishes is the best choice for a longer lasting finish, especially when using pine. I prefer California-brand paints for their durability and good coverage. They are also very easy to work with. Some woods, such as redwood, teak, and cedar, are rot-resistant and will hold up with a stain finish. We are not using them here because they can be expensive, hard to obtain, and difficult to carve. If you still want to stain your finished piece, you will have to apply a few coats of a marine or "spar" varnish after the stain and before applying the paint to the letters, bevel, and leaves and berries. You will have to reapply the varnish every 3-6 months after that, which ends up giving the whole sign a yellowish glaze.

## PAINT

In order to create some beautiful results for this and future projects, having some basic colors in latex and lettering enamels is essential. A huge variety of colors can be mixed from just a few. You can also buy any color, mixed for your needs, as well. Good basic colors include: white, black, a primary red (crimson is the name of a good premixed color), a bright yellow, blue, and tan.

Lettering oils are available in pint-sized cans. Basic colors (from *www.1shot.com*): white, bright red, reflex blue, black, and chrome yellow medium.

**1 Sand the sign.** Sand the edges of the sign and wipe dust off with a tack cloth. Always sand the edges of any sign to have a slightly rounded edge. This will weather better than if left sharp—paint will not cover that sharp edge well enough to last.

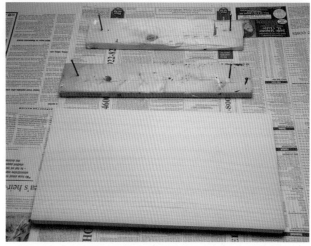

**2 Create drying stands.** You will need two scrap pieces of wood around 1' (305mm) long or so, with two finish nails hammered in each. Using a paint roller, prime the back of the sign. Don't prime the edges. Turn the sign over onto the drying stands.

**3 Prime the front.** Begin priming the carved numbers and chip carvings with a brush. Take care not to leave any puddles of paint in the carved crevasses. Finish by rolling primer on the face and edges. Let this coat dry thoroughly and repeat with at least two more coats.

## PAINTING THE SIGN

Two different types of paint are used in the finishing of an exterior sign. Exterior latex paint is used for the body or background of the sign, as well as any scene or artwork on the sign. Lettering is painted with a sign painter's enamel (a shiny oil-based paint) for contrast and durability. There are many brands of latex paint on the market, but, as stated before, I prefer California brand exterior latex, having had great results with this product. I used One Shot sign painter's enamel with great results for many years as well.

Choosing what colors to use can be a difficult task for many people. You can make this less challenging by answering a few basic questions: Will this sign hang on a wall or building? If so, what color is it? Are there any other accent colors on the building or in the room (shutters, trim, doors)? You want the finished piece to compliment the surroundings, not stick out like a sore thumb.

In this case, my circa board will go on my house, which is a light grey-green. My door and shutters are a burnt orange-red, and my trim is off-white. I will paint the body of the sign the same off-white as my trim, since the sign will go against the grey-green house, and paint the berries a similar burnt-orangey red to match the shutters. The green leaves will compliment the house color. I will paint the letters and the bevel darker and lighter tones of green as well. Choose paint colors to match the house you'll be fixing the sign to.

## BRUSHES

You will need several different types of brushes to paint the projects in this book. There are two main types of brushes: natural, meaning that the bristles are animal hair; and synthetic, meaning that the bristles are man-made. Most of the brushes you need for these projects will be synthetic. To help you understand the great variety of brushes available, I will give you a run-down of different kinds of brushes and their uses.

Note: You can spend a lot of money on brushes, but I recommend you buy a good middle-of-the-road quality. The examples pictured in this sidebar are good brands. The most important thing when selecting brushes is to be sure the ferrule, the metal part of the brush that wraps around the top of the bristles and the brush handle, is a fused solid piece without a seam.

Rounds feature a nice round tuft of bristles. Rounds are good basic brushes that come in a variety of sizes. They are the workhorses of brushes—you will use them most of all, so it's a good idea to get a selection of sizes. The pictured rounds are all synthetic brushes.

Flats have a thin, flat bunch of bristles. They are useful for many painting techniques, including line details and dry brushing.

Script liners, or quills, are used for letter painting, thin lines, and detailing. They differ from other brushes in the length of the bristle—often two or more times longer.

Blenders come in a variety of sizes. I prefer natural bristle blenders because the bristles don't clump as much as the synthetic version. The bristles are coarser, tend to have a firmer rounded tip, and they spread out a little to give an even blending effect.

**Mixing Tan**

If you have only the basic colors, make tan by mixing 3 parts yellow with a little less than 1 part red and a touch black. If the tan looks too greenish, adjust by adding a tiny amount of red. Likewise, if the mix looks too red, add a tiny amount of black.

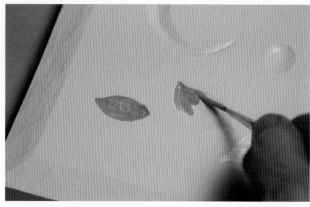

**1 Paint the body of the sign.** The first step is to paint the body of the sign with the off-white trim color, at least 3 coats, using the same method as when priming the sign.

**2 Base coat the leaves.** I want these leaves to be two tones of a sage green. Mix 3 parts yellow to 3 parts black, with a touch of white, to get the sage green I am using here. Take a portion of that color and mix an equal amount of white to achieve the lighter tone. Using a #2 or #4 script liner, base coat all the leaves with the light sage green.

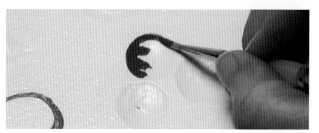

**3 Basecoat the stems.** Using a #1 or #2 script liner, basecoat the stems with the tan color. Most novice painters are afraid to use script liners because they don't think they can control these long bristles! Actually, the opposite is true. This brush doesn't react to an unsteady hand as quickly as a shorter brush, so your lines are straighter. Script liners also hold more paint—so you don't have as many stop and start marks. Holding your breath while you paint a line can help make a smoother line, too.

**4 Base coat the berries.** Use the California-brand tomahawk color mixed 1-1 with yellow to base coat the berries. You can make the tomahawk shade by mixing 1½ parts red with 2 parts yellow and a touch of black and white. Use a #4 or #6 round synthetic brush to paint the berries. First, paint carefully around the inside border of the berries. Gradually fill in the center with smooth strokes.

## BASE COATS

In order to cover the leaves and berries, a base coat must be applied. This is simply a coat of paint that goes underneath the final color in order to transition from the color of the sign to the final color, making that color bolder. It is usually a light or medium version of the final color choice. You can see that in the top picture, as the first coat of paint doesn't cover the white background completely. The bottom picture shows the leaf when it is finished, with the two tones of sage green blended into an opaque final coat—thanks to the base coat.

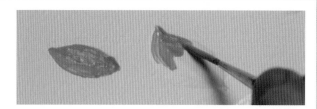

Base coat.

Final paint shade.

**5** **Allow the paint to dry.** At this time, allow the base coats to dry for 2–4 hours. Save your paints by covering the palette with plastic wrap. Be sure to flatten the wrap onto the paint to completely remove any air—paint will dry if it comes in contact with air. Doing this will keep your paint usable for at least 1 day.

## Fixing a Painting Mistake

If you do make a mistake by going outside the line, or need to clean up some paint on the sign, use clean water when using latex paints (or thinner when using oil-based paints) on a stiff brush. Wipe the brush on a rag so the brush is wet but not dripping, and push the misplaced paint the into area just painted. You may have to repeat this a few times. Never wipe the paint away from the painted area—you will just end up with a messy smudge to clean. Once the area is free of paint, carefully clean the area with a baby wipe. This will remove any haze left by the thinner.

Apply the two colors.

Tap the border.

Finished leaves.

**6** **Finish painting the leaves.** When the base coat is dry, apply the final blended coat of paint to the leaves and berries. Blending tones on an object gives depth and detail—it makes the difference between an amateur attempt and a professionally finished work, and it is really very easily accomplished with a little patience and practice. Paint the two tones of latex sage green on the leaf. Blend the two colors by patting or tapping the border between the colors repeatedly with the blender brush, jumping back and forth across the color border until the line separating them is gone. In other words, you should not be able to see a line where one color begins and another ends—they should gradually and smoothly flow into one another. Switch to a smaller round blender and pat or tap the edges of the leaf, being careful to keep the paint off the background sign color. If you do get some of the leaf green on the sign background, use a damp clean brush to scrub it off, pushing the green back into the leaf, not out into the sign.

**7** **Finish painting the stems.** Using the script liner, paint a second coat of tan on the stems. Without cleaning the brush, apply a little white paint to the script liner and mix to make a light tan. Brush this on the middle section of the stem to create a highlight. Using the light tan, continue the stem line about three-quarters of the way into the leaf center as a vein.

8 **Shade the berries.** Mix the tomahawk with yellow to make a light orange. Paint the upper left of the berry with this color, using a small #4 round. Paint the rest of the berry with straight tomahawk. Now, blend the two tones together with your blender brush.

9 **Add white highlights.** With a #4 blender brush, tap a little white paint in the upper left at the 10 o'clock position to give the berry a highlight. Finish the rest of the berries in the same way.

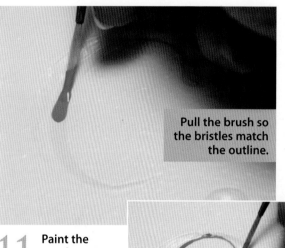

**Pull the brush so the bristles match the outline.**

10 **Mix the paint for the numbers and edges.** To create the darker color for the edge, use enamels to mix 1½ parts yellow to 2 parts black and ½ part white. Add 2½ parts more white to the dark mix to create the lighter tone.

**Switch directions as needed.**

11 **Paint the numbers.** Begin by painting the lighter sage in the letter c, using the smaller #2 script liner. Pull the brush along the edge, and the rest of the letter will fill in. Don't be afraid to switch directions if needed. Fill in any remaining white space as you go. Paint the numbers in the same way.

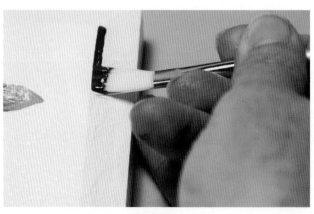

12 **Paint the beveled edge.** Use your pinky to guide the brush. Hold the flat letter brush as shown. I am using a long-bristle ¼" (6mm) flat brush here. Paint the straight edge of the top of the bevel by using your pinky finger as a guide, keeping your hand stiff, and pulling the brush along the edge. Paint in the rest of the beveled edge. You have completed the carving and painting of the first sign!

CHAPTER 2:

# WELCOME SIGN

This is a great project that will introduce a few new skills and doubles as a beautiful adornment for your home or as a gift for a lucky friend! A flower motif is a favorite for house signs, and this lily will be a great way to illustrate the method used to chip-carve a more complex design with layers. The step-by-step painting instructions will build on the previous lesson, using the same techniques, but giving you some experience in painting a more detailed design.

## NEW TOPICS IN THIS CHAPTER

> Gluing and cutting a sign blank
> Chip carving a more complex design
> Painting a more complex image

# MATERIALS & TOOLS

- (2) Boards, 1¼" x 4½" x 18" (32mm x 114mm x 457mm)
- (4) C-clamps
- (2) Pipe clamps
- Glue, good-quality exterior, such as T-88 by System Three Resins, Inc.
- Cups and sticks to mix glue
- Plastic strips
- Scrap wood for clamping
- Rubber gloves (optional)
- Belt sander
- Pad sander
- Safety glasses
- Dust mask
- Band saw, saber saw, or coping saw
- Full-size pattern
- Pencil
- Ruler (see-thru with grids preferable)
- Carbon paper
- Square
- String, about 2' (610mm) long

# CHISELS NEEDED

I am giving you the "dream list" of chisels for this project—please note that you can substitute a chisel of the same number but with a smaller mm size if you don't have the size I mention.

#1 12mm skew; #2 8mm; #2 12mm; #2 16mm; #3 16mm; #3 20mm; #5 3mm; #5 5mm; #5 8mm; #5 20mm; #7 10mm; #7 14mm; #8 7mm; #9 10mm; #11 7mm; #13 10mm V-groove; #15 6mm V-groove

**Complete Welcome
Sign Pattern**
Photocopy at 200%.

Arrows indicate starting points
Lines indicate stopping points
Red lines indicate stop cuts
Thicken letters before tracing

## CREATING THE BLANK

In order to carve signs in a variety of shapes and sizes, you will need large blanks composed of a number of pieces of wood. You may be able to find someone to do this for you, but it is cheaper and faster to do it yourself.

1 **Choose the boards.** When choosing the wood for a project, inspect it to be sure it is free of warping, knots, sap pockets, checks, and cracks. Glue two pieces of 1¼" x 4½" x 18" (32mm x 114mm x 457mm) wood to form a sign blank with a final size of 1¼" x 9" x 18" (32mm x 229mm x 457mm). Prime the end grain to keep the moisture content more stable. Since 80–90% of the moisture in wood enters and leaves through the end grain, sealing it will help prevent warping and splitting.

2 **Orient the boards.** It is important to have the growth rings (the dark and light bands on the end grain) placed so they are the reverse of each other. This will help prevent warping. As shown, the growth rings (drawn here for clarity) are the reverse of one another.

3 **Assemble gluing materials.** Gather all needed materials for gluing: C-clamps, bar clamps, scrap wood, cups and sticks for mixing glue, plastic strips, and glue. You need a good exterior glue for any signs that are going to end up outside. I have used a product called T-88, made by System Three Resins, Inc., for many years with great results. It is a bit expensive, but you are better off spending the money now and preventing the glue seam failure later. Be sure to read all safety warnings and advice on their website, *www.systemthree.com*, before using.

5 **Apply the glue.** If you're using T-88, this is how you prepare it. Pour an equal amount (about ⅛ cup each) of parts A and B into plastic cups. Do not use metal containers. Pour together. Mix with a stick until the color changes to a creamy off-white. Spread the glue on one surface only of the wood edge to be glued. Cover the scraps of wood with plastic strips. Lay the wood down and push the boards together by hand.

4 **Set up to glue.** After assembling all the materials for gluing, prepare a spot where the blank can remain in the clamps for 24–36 hours undisturbed. Spread some newspapers on the surface for easy clean up-later. Put the boards in the pipe clamps and bring up the bottom of the clamps so they are close to the wood, as shown.

**6** **Adjust the clamps.** Bring up the bottom portions of the pipe clamps to fit snuggly against the bottom of the blank. The top of the blank should be tight to the top of the clamp. Line up the edges of the boards to one another. This will save squaring them up later. Place a piece of scrap wood with a plastic strip under and on top of both edges. Tighten the pipe clamps until some glue oozes out of the joint. Do not starve the joint by over-tightening. Make the clamps snug but not really tight. Put two C-clamps on each end. These will keep the sign blank flat. When done, be sure to go back to the pipe clamps to see if they are very snug—sometimes they loosen up a bit.

**7** **Sand the sign blank.** Grab a belt sander, pad sander, safety glasses, and dust mask. Take the blank out of the clamps when the glue is dry and solid to the touch—generally between 24–36 hours. Use a bench with a stop or bench dogs on it to prevent the blank from kicking out when using the sander. Use the belt sander with a 60-grit belt, followed by an 80-grit belt. Be sure to follow all safety suggestions on your sander, and wear goggles. Sand both sides. Follow up with the pad sander with 100-grit sandpaper.

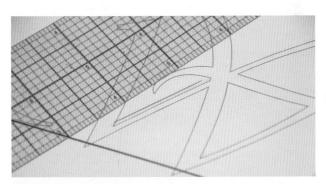

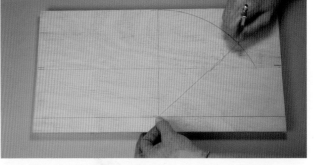

**8** **Prepare the design.** Using a triangle, check to see if the sides of the blank are square to the bottom. If it is not, it needs to be cut square. I suggest using a table saw. Copy the pattern on page 34. You may wish to thicken some portions of the letters to make them easier to carve. If so, use a see-through ruler to fatten the thinner legs of the letters. Since many of the computer-generated fonts have to be adjusted, it's useful to know how to do this.

**9** **Draw the outline.** Draw the centerline from top to bottom. Also, scribe the letter line 1" (25mm) up from the bottom. Measure up 4½" (114mm) from the bottom on the left and right edges and mark. Cut a string 20" (508mm) long. Tie a loop in one end of the string. Put your pencil through the loop onto the top center point. With your other hand, pull the string tight and line up the string with the centerline. Place your thumbnail on the string at the point where it intersects the letter line and hold firmly. Keeping the pull with the pencil steady and firm, draw the arc to the right to the mark 4½" (114mm) up. Repeat to the left. Use a round object (a can, a plate, a protractor) to draw in the curve at the shoulder of the sign.

**10** **Trace the design onto the board.** Trace on the letters, lining them up on the letter line and centering them as you did in Chapter 1 (page 12). Trace the lily in the rounded part of the sign. Because the lily's design is pretty symmetrical, you can fold it in half to find the center. After lining up the fold line of the lily to the centerline on the sign, you can raise or lower it as you please, but be sure to keep it a minimum of ½" (13mm) from the top to prevent chipping. Number the leaves and petals as shown on the pattern.

# CARVE THE *W*

Although we will be carving letters rather than numbers in this project, the same principles apply. We will not repeat the basic letter carving done in Chapter 1. Instead, we will cover carving the *W* as well as the *m* in "Welcome" since they are more advanced and complex. As in Project 1, be sure to clamp the sign blank to the bench.

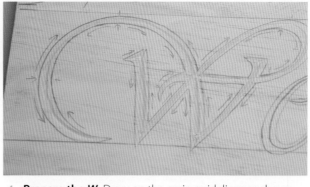

**1** **Prepare the *W*.** Draw on the grain guidelines as shown. Stop-cut the guidelines with the #13 10mm V-groove.

**2** **Carve the inner left curve.** Using a #2 12mm chisel, start carving at the arrow of the inner curve of the left hand curl on the W. Continue down and to the left until you reach the midpoint halfway down. Starting at the tip of the curl, carve the inner curve up in the direction of the arrow with the same chisel. Blend into the previous cut.

**3** **Carve the outside curve on the left.** Now, using a #5 20mm chisel, begin carving the outer curve on the left, starting at the arrow and continuing up to the top of the curve. Repeat from the midpoint arrow and carve the outer curve down to the tip.

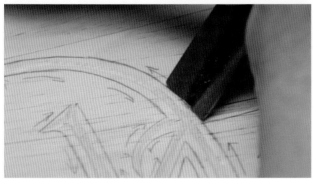

**4** **Carve the outer part of the loop.** With the same chisel, start at the midpoint of the curve (at the intersection of the right loop) and carve the outer curve on the right up to the top. Blend into the last cut.

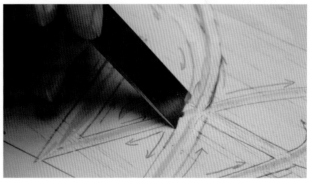

**5** **Carve the inner part of the loop.** Now repeat the cut on the inner curve with the #2 12mm chisel from the top of the curve down to the right and continue in the direction of the arrow until you reach the bottom point of that leg.

**6** **Carve up the long leg.** With the same chisel, proceed up the other side of the same leg of the letter until you reach the intersection of the right loop. Switch back to the #5 20mm chisel to continue cleaning the letter after the intersection.

7 **Cut the top left serif.** With the corner of the #2 12mm, cut the angle of the serif on the leg of the *W*. Cut the curve of the serif with the corner of the #2 as well.

8 **Cut down the left leg.** Carve the rest of the leg with the #2 chisel down to the point, and then carve the other side of this leg as well.

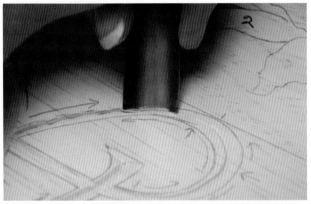

9 **Cut up the center left leg.** Continue with the same #2 12mm up the second thinner leg in the direction of the arrow. Switch to the #3 20mm chisel, and then the #5 20mm, as you continue carving this edge up to the top of the loop's curve in the direction of the arrows.

10 **Carve the inside of the big right loop.** With the #2 12mm chisel, begin at the centerpoint of the inner curve of this loop and continue carving down to the left, in the direction of the arrow, past the intersection of lines to the bottom of the point.

11 **Carve the tail end of the right loop.** With the #7 14mm chisel, begin carving the top of the tail end of the right loop that intersects at the center of the *W*. Switch to the #2 8mm to carve the lower curve.

12 **Carve the outer right curve.** With the #7 14mm chisel, carve the outer curve of the loop on the right side of the letter. Continue up in the direction of the arrow and blend into the previous cut. Bring the chisel back to the arrow at the midpoint of the loop and carve down in the direction of the arrow. As the curve becomes less tight, switch to a #5 20mm and continue.

13 **Carve the bottom and top of the straight part of the right loop.** As the letter straightens out, switch to the #2 12 or 16mm chisel. Continue across to join the previous cut. With the same chisel, carve the top of this line and continue in the direction of the arrow, switching to a smaller #2 8mm when the curve starts to tighten. Continue to the midpoint at the arrow.

14 **Carve the remaining inside right loop.** With the same #2 8mm chisel, start at the top of the inner curve and continue down in the direction of the arrow. Blend in with the previous cut.

15 **Cut the rightmost serif.** With the corner of the same chisel, carve the top of the serif. Carve the curve of the serif, as well.

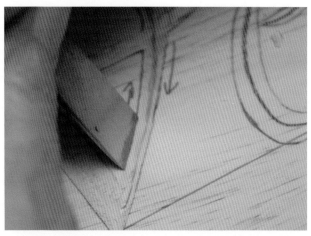

16 **Carve the right side of the rightmost leg.** With a #5 8mm chisel, carve the right side of the rightmost leg. Switch to a #5 20mm to carve the rest of this curve. Switch to a #2 16mm to carve the straight portion of the line; continue to the bottom point.

17 **Carve the left side of the rightmost leg.** Using a #2 16mm, carve up the opposite side of this leg and finish at the top of the leg, blending the cut into the previous ones. Clean any parts of the *W* that need it.

# Making the Welcome Sign

## CARVE THE *M*

1 **Carve the upper left serif.** Draw on the grain guidelines as shown. Carve the stop cuts with the #13 10mm V-groove. Use the corner of the #2 12mm to carve the end of the serif.

2 **Carve the left side of the left leg.** Using the same #2, start at the lower point of the first leg. Carve up in the direction of the arrow to the top of the leg.

3 **Carve the right side of the left leg.** With the #5 8mm chisel, carve the curve on the opposite side of the top of the leg. After carving the curved top of the leg, switch to the #2 12mm and continue to carve down the letter leg to the bottom. Clean the angled bottom with the same chisel.

4 **Carve the top of the left hump.** With the #3 16mm, begin carving the thin connector line on the outer left curve of the left hump. Switch to the outer right curve of the left hump and carve this with the same chisel. With the #8 7mm chisel, carve the tight outer curve at the top of the left hump.

5 **Carve the inside of the left hump.** Using the #2 8mm, begin at the top inner curve of the letter and continue down to the left. Join the cuts on the first leg of the *m*. Clean from the top side with the #3 16mm.

6 **Carve the left side of the middle leg.** Begin carving the second, or middle, leg of the *m* with a #2 12mm chisel. Start as before at the lower left point of the leg and continuing up to the top of the leg. Use the #7 14mm to clean the top outer curve of the middle leg.

**7** **Carve the right side of the middle leg.** Switch to the #2 12mm chisel and continue carving the straight portion of the middle leg down to the bottom. Since the remainder of the letter is the same as the first part, you can continue to carve the rest of the *m* by repeating steps 2–6. Because the rest of the letters repeat former lessons, (for example, the *e* and *o* are very similar to the *c* in the circa board), I will not repeat them here. Go on to finish carving and cleaning the rest of the letters.

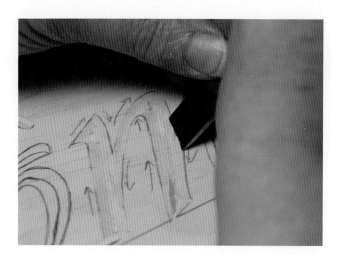

## ALTERNATE LETTER CARVING METHOD

It is possible, but a little more difficult, to carve these letters using just the #13 10mm V-groove.

To the right is part of the *e* in the sign carved with just the #13. Note the smooth, non-textured sides. This method of carving does not have the facets of the traditional method I have been showing you. Some people like the facets, since they add a hand-carved effect and, when gold leaf is applied, the facets enhance the overall effect. Here are the basics of carving with just the #13.

The *e*.

**1** **Cut the left side of the letter.** Use only the left-hand side of the chisel to cut the left side of the letter and push up, carving with the grain.

**2** **Carve the right side of the letter.** Now, approaching from the top of the letter, cut the right side of the letter with only the right side of the chisel, carving down the letter with the grain. With practice, and being sure to switch direction based on the grain direction, you can carve any letter with this method.

## CHIP CARVING THE LILY

The lily will be chip carved in progressive steps, following the order indicated by the numbers on each portion. Begin with the elements labeled "1" and then "2" and so on, stop-cutting first where indicated. You will note that the stop cuts are used to separate one leaf or petal from another where they overlap. Never stop-cut the outer edges.

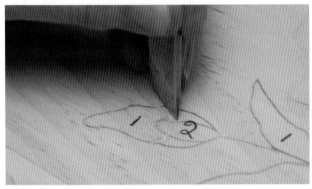

1 **Stop-cut the bud.** Begin by stop-cutting the lines separating the 1 from the 2 with the #15 6mm V-groove. Using the #1 12mm skew, stop-cut the inner corners of the bud that the V-groove can't reach.

2 **Scoop the bud out.** With the #11 7mm, begin scooping the bud from the tip into the stop cut separating the bud from the leaves. Use the left side of the chisel to scoop the upper edge of the bud, and scoop the lower edge of the bud with the right side of the chisel.

3 **Clean out the bud's corners.** Use the #1 12mm skew to recut the inner corners of the bud and then a #5 3mm to clean out the small chips. You'll do a final cleaning at the end of the chip carving to catch any stray chips, but the bud is done for now. Repeat steps 2–3 for the bud on the right side.

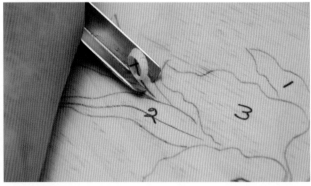

4 **Stop-cut the two remaining "1" areas on the left.** Move on to stop cut the two leaves on the left side that are labeled with the number 1. I suggest using the #13 10mm V-groove. Use the 12mm skew to make any small stop cuts the V-groove can't reach.

TIP

**Where Not To Stop Cut**
Never ever stop cut the outer edges of a chip carving. The only edges that will be stop cut are the ones that are next to other elements.

Stop cuts for lily.

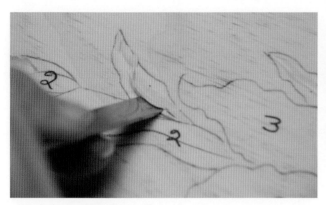

**5** **Carve both sides of the leaf.** Using the #5 8mm chisel, begin carving at an angle into the stop cut from the edge of the leaf. Start on the top left, and continue carving down to the base of the leaf. Start at the opposite side of the base and carve into the stop cut. Continue up the leaf, carving with the grain, to the other end of the leaf. Carve the rest of the leaves labeled #1 in the same way.

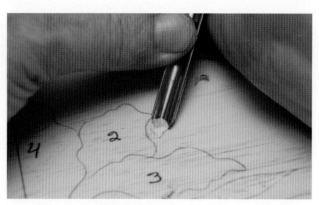

**6** **Scoop out petal curl "1."** Scoop out the curl labeled "1" in the petal labeled #2 with the #11 7mm chisel, using the two sides of the chisel to carve the sides of the petal curl. Start the first cut on the bottom and then carve up the left side. Be sure to use the left side of the chisel. Start the second cut on the top. Carve down the right side.

**7** **Carve the bud leaf area.** With the #11 7mm chisel, begin scooping each side of the bud's leaves. Scoop out the center with the same chisel. Carefully shave the area near the stop cut, being sure to leave the edges slightly higher than the bud.

**8** **Stop-cut and carve leaf "2," on the left side.** Use the same techniques as you did on the previous leaves. Carve the stop cut first. Use a #5 8mm chisel to carve from the top edge of the leaf to the stop cut. As you get close to the intersection with the lily, use a smaller area of the chisel to be more precise. Repeat this process on the "2" leaf on the right side of the lily.

**9** **Carve the "2" petal.** Using the #15 6mm V-groove and the skew, stop cut the line between the #2 petal and the petals next to it. Using the #11 7mm chisel, begin scooping the petal, working toward the stop cut at the base. The finished petal should be about ⅛–¼" (3mm–6mm) deep.

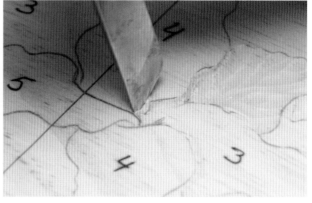

**10** **Stop-cut petal "3" on the right.** Begin stop-cutting the petal labelled 3 on the right side. Stop-cut the areas that the V-groove can't reach with the skew. You can also use the #5 5mm chisel to cut in a stop cut when needed.

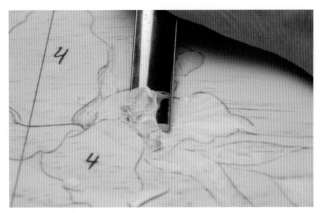

**11** **Carve petal "3" on the right.** Begin scooping this petal in the same manner as the first. Continue working your way to the stop cuts, scooping from the outer edge into the center. In the wider parts of the petal, use the #7 10mm chisel to scoop. Use the chisel edge to cut the wood chips free of the stop cut line.

**12** **Stop-cut the petal "3" on the left.** For the petal "3" on the left side, stop-cut the line between petal "3" and petal "4," and the line between the petal "3" and petal "5." Use a #15 6mm V-groove for this. Use the skew to stop cut any tight angle.

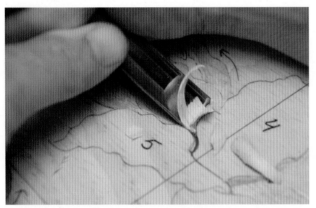

**13** **Carve petal "3" on the left side.** Begin scooping this petal with the #11 7mm. Scoop with the larger #7 14mm in the wider portions of the petal, cutting right into the stop cut.

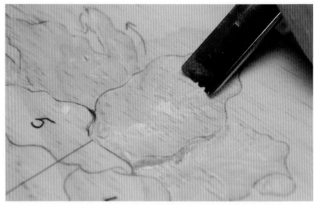

**14** **Carve the top petal "4."** Begin stop-cutting and scooping the "4" petal at the top of the sign. Scoop out the top of the petal with the #9 10mm chisel. Switch to a larger #7 14mm chisel in wider sections, scooping toward the center of the petal. Repeat this for the other petal labeled "4."

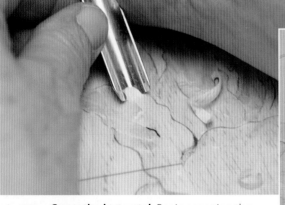

**15** **Carve the last petal.** Begin scooping the last petal, labelled "5," using the #8 7mm chisel or the #11 7mm. Switch to the larger #9 10mm chisel where needed.

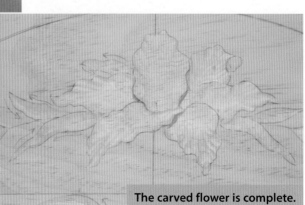

**The carved flower is complete.**

# CUTTING OUT THE SHAPE ON THE BAND SAW

The band saw is a versatile and essential tool in any wooden sign shop, enabling the user to cut straight or curved shapes with ease. Whenever using any power tool, always be sure to read and follow the safety precautions advised by the manufacturer. Always wear safety goggles and ear protection, and be sure to use your band saw in a well-lit area. Be sure there is nothing and no one near to distract you while cutting. Keep your full attention on the blade. We will now cut out the top shape of the sign, following the pencil curves drawn earlier. If a band saw is unavailable to you, substituting a saber saw or coping saw would be an alternative, but will not give as clean and precise a cut.

1 **Line up the cut.** Turn on the saw. Place the signboard on the table and slowly push it toward the saw blade, lining up the pencil line with the blade. Be sure to keep hands and fingers well away from the blade.

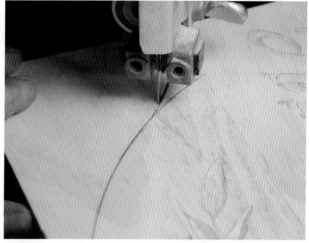

2 **Cut the top shape.** Push the sign blank slowly into the blade, taking care not to force the cut—let the blade do the work. Gently begin turning the blank little by little to cut the arc. Carefully cut the top arc as precisely as possible; this will save you from sanding to correct the shape later.

3 **Sand the sign.** Use the pad sander with an 80-grit paper, followed by a 100-grit paper, to sand the sides and edges of the sign to smooth and slightly round them. Wipe the sign clean. You're ready to paint.

## PREPARING THE WELCOME SIGN FOR PAINTING

As in Chapter 1, we will begin by priming the sanded and dust-free carved sign with three coats of latex primer, using the same technique outlined in that chapter. The primer will seal the wood and provide a bonding surface for the finish coats of paint.

### COLORS NEEDED FOR THIS SIGN

Note: All latex colors used in this project and others in this book, unless otherwise specified, are California Brand Exterior Latex. All specific paint names and numbers refer to that brand.

- Background color: elm court #8595D, a grayish blue-green

- Forest green

- A special mix of bright yellow, (formula T-12y—this is used by the paint store to mix that specific shade)

- Tomahawk #7856A

- Nu-white

**1 Prime the sign.** Prime the sign following the method detailed in Chapter 1 (page 27).

**2 Apply a basecoat to the sign.** Apply a basecoat to the entire sign. I have chosen a dark tone of grayish blue-green (Elm Court) for the background.

**3 Base coat the flower and leaves.** I want to paint the lily with the same colors as in the reference photo at right. The lily in the example is mostly white with some pink, so I'll base coat it with white. Two coats of white are needed to cover the darker color of the sign's background paint. The leaves are painted with a light green.

This is part of a larger commercial sign I did for a florist a few years ago. The lily is basically white with pink, so I will base coat it with white.

**4 Base coat the letters.** After base coating the sign, choose an oil-based enamel sign painter's paint for the letters. I have chosen a pale yellow, to pick up the eventual yellow center of the flower. Look back to page 31 for more detail on base coating letters.

# PAINTING THE LILY

I have chosen a pale peach with darker shadows for the lily. We will be blending these two colors and then adding some details to enhance the finished flower. I used a photo of a lily from my own garden as reference. I want to stress the importance of reference materials for whatever you are painting (or carving)—photos, other paintings, etc. A note about copyrights—it's fine to use a copyrighted piece of artwork for your carving or painting; just understand you cannot sell it, since it is someone else's work, without their permission. Giving it as a gift or for your own use is fine. Painting seems to be a stumbling block for most carvers, but carving a beautiful piece only to rush through the painting is a shame.  By spending a little time practicing these steps—from base coating to blending—you will have a piece that you will be so proud of!

---

## PRACTICE: BLENDING

In this project, we will be doing some more advanced blending than in Chapter 1. Blending and shading any painting, whether on wood or canvas, is the key to creating a well-done, dimensional, and professional piece.

**1 Paint two tones.** Paint two tones to be blended side by side. Both colors need to be wet to blend properly. Don't be afraid to use a good amount of paint—the blending will be easier.

**2 Position the blending brush.** Position the blending brush with half of the bristles in one color, and half in the other. Refer to Chapter 1 for photos and a list of blending brushes (page 28).

**3 Tap the brush.** Begin tapping the brush into the paint. This will mix the edges of the two colors. Don't be afraid to "jump" back and forth over the border of the colors to blend well. You are done blending only when you can no longer see a line where the two colors separate.

Finished effect of the blending.

**1** **Mix the paint for the leaves.** Apply some white, yellow, and forest green on some tin foil (or palette paper if you prefer). Gather some water, brushes, and a cloth for cleaning brushes. Mix 2 parts yellow to 1 part forest green to make a medium green. Take some of this medium green and mix 1 part white to 1 part medium green to make a light green. You will use these two colors to paint the leaf at the base of the bud.

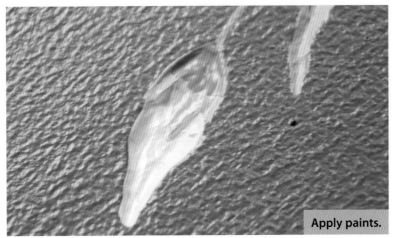

Apply paints.

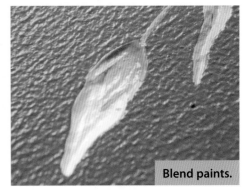

Blend paints.

**2** **Paint the bud leaves.** Paint the zigzag side of the bud leaf with the lightest green, and the rest with the medium green. Blend. Paint the other bud leaf.

**3** **Paint the leaves.** Pick a leaf to paint. Apply forest green at the base, the medium green in the center, and the light green at the tip. Blend. Paint all the leaves on the sign in this manner. Note: Occasionally, a second coat may be needed to provide good coverage. I did apply a second coat to the leaves, using the same blending method, after I finished painting the lily.

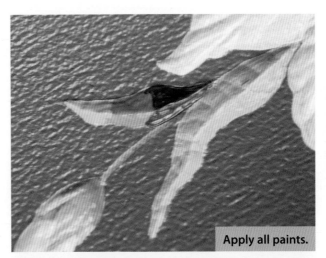

Apply all paints.

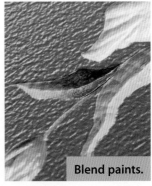

Blend paints.

**4** **Paint the buds.** Mix a pink tone by using tomahawk and white. Mix 1 part white to 2 parts tomahawk. Paint the tip of the bud white and the base of the bud the light tomahawk mix. Blend as shown. Paint the other bud.

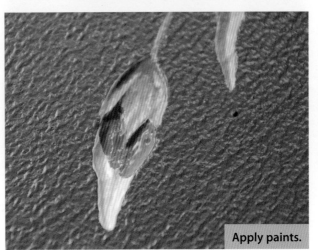

Apply paints.

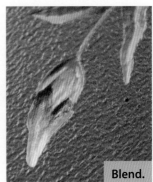

Blend.

Apply paints to petal "1."

Blend petal "1."

5 **Paint the petals.** Paint the edges of the petal with white. Paint the center portion of the petal with the light tomahawk mix. Blend the white and pink mix as shown. Proceed to paint and blend each petal of the lily in the same order you carved them in. Only proceed to the next petal when the blending is done. Study the photos closely to see where I apply the paint on each petal. I recommend applying the pink mixture most heavily to the base of the petal and tapering off down the center. Blend from the center outward.

Apply paints to petal "2."

Blend petal "2" and paint petal "3."

Blend petal "3."

TIP

**Dark and Light Tones**

Dark tones and light tones of color serve to control dimension in a painting. A darker tone will push the object, or part of an object, backward, causing it to recede. A lighter tone brings things forward. This simple principal is what gives every painted object dimension. Look at the photo of the finished blending and notice how the lighter edges of the petals pop off the darker pink when they overlap one another.

Paint petal "4."

Blend petal "4."

Paint petal "5."

Blend petal "5" and apply paint to petal "6."

Blend petal "6."

Completed blending on the lily and leaves.

# DETAIL PAINTING THE LILY

Once the petals are blended from dark to light, we will paint the details on the flower. Be sure to complete this step—the little bit of effort needed will pay off in the finished product. Wait to apply the detail elements until the last coats of paint are completely dry—that way, if you do make a mistake, you can simply wipe the paint off with a damp cloth and try again.

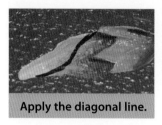
**Apply the diagonal line.**

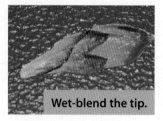
**Wet-blend the tip.**

1 **Detail the buds.** Dampen the tip of the bud with water—dampen, not soak. Use a #1 script liner with straight Tomahawk to paint a thin stripe diagonally across the bud, in an *S*-curve as shown. Blend the line into the dampened tip, taking care to leave some of the line. Detail the other bud.

2 **Detail the bud leaves.** Using the water blending technique described at left, blend some forest green on the base of the bud leaves. Now, using the same green, pull up a few lines from the base of the leaves as shown. Use a #1 script liner brush.

3 **Add pink to the petals.** Apply a small amount of the straight tomahawk paint to the center of the base of each petal (petal 1 shown here). Using the water-blending technique, blend this color into the petal as shown. Repeat this process on each petal.

**Add paint.**

**Wet-blend the paint.**

**All petals wet-blended.**

**4** **Add light yellow to the petals.** Now mix a light yellow—1 part yellow to 3 parts white. Use a script liner to paint a long line, thicker at the bottom and thinner at the top, up the center of the petal. Using the same script liner, pull a few whispy lines from the center and out, as shown. Repeat for all the petals. Use a script liner to paint dark green lines down the middle of the leaves.

Paint on light yellow.

Pull out a few whispy lines.

The light yellow applied on all petals.

**5** **Add brighter yellow accents.** Thin the yellow with a little water. Blend some at the base of the light yellow center detail as shown.

Use the handle tip to make dots.

Use a wet brush to remove bad spots.

6 **Add dots to the petals.** Mix equal parts yellow, forest green, and tomahawk to make a medium brown. Using the end of a paintbrush handle, dot the petals. If you wish to remove a dot that is too large, simply take a wet brush and carefully wash it off. You may have to repeat this to completely remove it.

7 **Paint the stamens.** Using the same brown, paint 2 or 3 lines from the center of the flower and add elongated dots to the tops as shown. You've now completed the flower and the sign.

Paint stamens.

Finished sign.

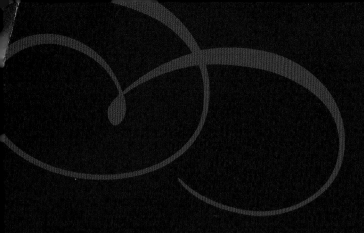

# CHAPTER 3:
# HOUSE SIGN
## with Applied Cap and Molding

There will be a time when you want to create a sign with either your name or someone else's. In order to create a sign customized with whatever text you want, you have to choose one of two methods—draw them yourself, or use a computer program designed to work with fonts, which are different styles of lettering. Although you can enlarge and copy fonts you may find available, the creative possibilities open to you with a program designed to manipulate fonts are endless, and well worth the effort to buy and learn. I have had no formal computer or computer graphics training, and have been able to work with a software program called CorelDraw with great results. There are some free downloads available online as well.

For this project, we will need a blank measuring 18½" x 11" x 1½" (470mm x 279mm x 38mm) as well as a piece of molding 2' (610mm) long and a piece of pine 21½" x 2½" x ¾" (546mm x 64mm x 19mm). (Instructions for gluing up a sign blank are covered in Chapter 2). The pattern for the pineapple and fruit is on page 56, and can be enlarged for the carving. Note that there is also a pattern with the sign drawn with the pineapple pattern but no name. You can use this if you have a scanner available to create the sign layout.

## NEW TOPICS IN THIS CHAPTER

> Using a computer to generate curved lettering

> Chip carving a more complex grouping

> Painting a more complex group of objects

> Adding a raised cap and molding detail

# MATERIALS & TOOLS

- (1) Piece of pine 18½" x 11" x 1½" (470mm x 279mm x 38mm), for sign blank
- (1) Pine board 21½" x 2½" x ¾" (546mm x 64mm x 19mm)
- Molding, 24"x 1¼" or 1½" (610mm x 32mm or 38mm)
- String to draw curve
- Pencil
- Ruler
- Square
- Carbon
- Pattern
- Assorted chisels to carve letters and fruit pattern
- Band saw
- Drill
- Miter box
- Hammer
- Brads (nails), #16 1¼"
- Sandpaper
- Primer and brush
- Exterior latex paint (see Painting section for list of colors)
- Assorted artist paintbrushes

**Fruit Pattern**
Copy at 125%.

Center of design

Center of design

Arrows indicate starting points
Lines indicate stopping points
Red lines indicate stop cuts
Numbers indicate carving sequence

**Sign Blank Layout**

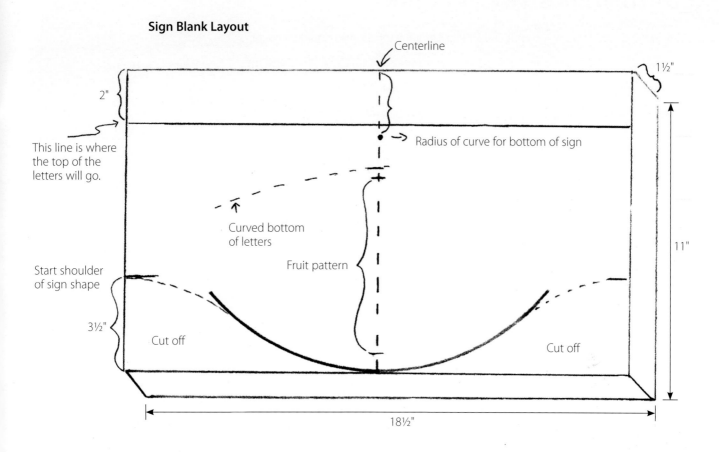

Centerline

1½"

2"

This line is where the top of the letters will go.

Radius of curve for bottom of sign

Curved bottom of letters

Fruit pattern

11"

Start shoulder of sign shape

3½"

Cut off

Cut off

18½"

1 Find and draw the centerline.

2 Measure down 2" (51mm) from the top for the top of the letter line.

3 Measure down 2⅜" (60mm) from the top for the radius point of the arc for the curve on the bottom of the sign.

4 Measure up 3½" (89mm) from the bottom on both sides for the shoulder of the curved bottom of the sign.

5 Measure up 7" (178mm) from the bottom— this is where the tip of the center leaf of the pineapple will be placed to transfer the design to the blank.

6 ⅜" (10mm) up from the tip of this leaf is where the bottom of the center letter will be.

## CUSTOMIZING THE PATTERN

There are a variety of ways you could take the pattern for this project and customize it for your use. I like to use CorelDraw 12 and my scanner to scan the pattern into my computer and then modify it and add text using CorelDraw. There are a number of computer programs that will do this, including Adobe Photoshop, Adobe Illustrator, and even Microsoft Word. Play around with the programs you have access to and see what works for you. You could also print out each letter separately and place them by hand on the desired curve; with a few minor adjustments, the letters will fit nicely. Of course, you can also draw the letters by hand if you are comfortable doing that. Use whatever method you desire to create the letters for your sign.

## CARVE THE SIGN

This project is a more complex chip carving. Follow the instructions and remember what you've learned in the previous projects; you'll soon have carved a sign you can be proud of!

**TIP**

### Cutting A Curved Edge
You can also use the chisel to cut a curved edge by matching the curve to cut to the curve of the chisel, as seen here.

1 **Lay out the sign.** Now that you have your pattern and the sign blank (18½" x 11" x 1¼"), you need to draw the shape. Draw all the measurements in the sketch above onto the sign blank. Using the radius point plotted on the centerline, draw an arc using the string method described in Chapter 2 (page 36). Next, draw on the "shoulders" of the sign using a round shape as in Chapter 2 (page 36). See page 57 for more instruction.

2 **Transfer the pattern.** After drawing on the guidelines and sign shape, position the letters and pattern on the sign and transfer using carbon paper.

3 **Carve the letters.** Carve the letters in the same manner detailed in Chapters 1 and 2. Also transfer the numbers showing the carving sequence to the design. Use a band saw to cut out the shape of the sign.

4 **Stop-cut the leaves labeled "1."** With the #13 10mm V-groove, stop-cut all the leaves labeled with a "1" and carve as detailed in Chapter 1 (page 26). Carve in the direction of the grain guidelines.

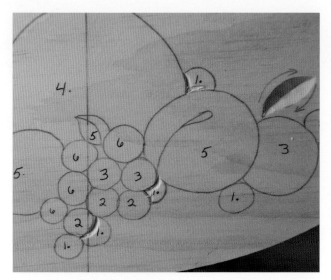

5 **Carve the "1" berries.** Stop-cut only those lines where the berry shape is "cut off," or seems to go below an object next to it, using a #15 6mm V-groove (and a skew for the corners). Carve these by scooping into the stop cut, using a #9 15mm and a #7 8mm fishtail. Now scoop all whole berries labeled "1" with the #9 15mm, switching to a smaller #7 8mm or 10mm chisel if needed.

6 **Carve all "2" elements.** Proceed to carve all elements labeled "2," stop-cutting where needed. Use a smaller #9 15mm chisel on the smaller berries to the right and center, switching to a larger #8 25mm for the larger fruit to the left. Use the skew and smaller #7 chisels to clean as detailed in Chapter 2 (page 40).

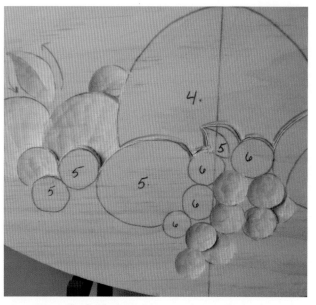

7 **Carve the "3" areas.** Stop-cut and scoop the larger "3" fruits on the right and left sides using a #7 14mm, and scoop the smaller berries in the center using the #9 15mm.

8 **Carve the "4" berry.** Stop-cut the smaller berry on the left labeled "4," and then proceed to the pineapple.

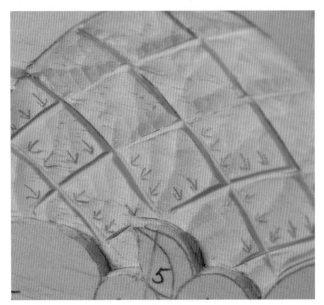

**9** **Carve the pineapple.** Stop-cut the bottom of the pineapple with the #15 6mm V-groove. Use the skew where needed in the corners. Scoop the pineapple into the stop cuts with the #8 25mm chisel, switching to a smaller #7 10mm where needed. Be careful around the "5" leaf—repeat the stop cut with the V-groove as you scoop. Draw diagonal lines on the pineapple as shown. Use your #15 6mm V-groove to cut a trench on the lines. Use a #5 8mm to slightly round the two lower edges of each diamond. Mark these areas with pencil to guide your carving.

**10** **Carve the "5" areas.** Stop-cut the "5" leaf as well as the line drawn on the peach on the right. Mark carving arrows on the peach to help with direction. Scoop out the fruit on the left with a #7 14mm. Carve the leaf with a #5 12mm. Scoop out the two berries on the left. Carve the upper part of the peach, cutting into the stop cut and scooping a trench around the top. Now, scoop out the larger area of the peach with a #7 14mm, leaving the area near the line. Using a #5 12mm, round over this line and scoop out a teardrop shape at the top with a #11 4mm.

**11** **Carve the "6" areas.** Scoop out the remaining berries marked with a 6 with the #9 15mm.

**12** **Complete the carving.** Clean up any stray wood chips in the carving. Finish by sanding the edges with a pad sander.

# MAKE THE CAP AND MOLDING

Adding a cap and molding is an option that gives a sign a more formal look. It is a Federalist style that would especially compliment a colonial home as well as many other traditional styles.

For this part, you need a 2' (610mm) length of molding that should not exceed 1½" (38mm) in width. You'll also need a ¾" (19mm) piece of pine, measuring 2½" x 24" (64mm x 610mm), for the cap. Make sure to also get a miter box, which will be used to cut a 45° angle on the molding.

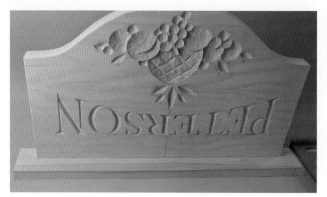

**2 Make the molding.** Cut the molding. Set the angle of the miter box to 45° left and cut the end of the molding. Note that the molding is upside down. Line up the angled cut of the molding to the front left sign corner as shown, and mark the other end of the molding at the opposite corner. Change the angle of the miter to 45° right and cut on the mark. You've completed the front molding; set it aside. Now cut the molding for the left side of the sign. Bring the remaining piece of molding to the left of the saw blade and cut, using the same 45° right angle. Fit this piece to the front piece of molding. Mark the molding where it meets the back of the sign. Use a square to mark the bottom of the molding to check for squareness. Change the angle of the miter to 90° and cut the left molding piece. Now change the angle of the miter to 45° left and cut the end off the molding. Now, fit the molding to the other side of the sign and mark as before. Cut at a 90° angle.

**1 Make the cap.** Position the cap. Place the sign upside down on the pine. Be sure to have the back of the sign flush with the edge of the cap. The cap will extend 1½" (38mm) out from the front of the sign. Use this same measure for the cap at the left and right sides as well. The length of the cap should be 21½" (546mm). Set the saw angle in the miter box at 90°. Hold the pine firmly braced against the back of the saw base and cut the cap to length. Measure and draw a centerline on the cap.

**3 Attach the cap and molding.** In order to glue and nail the cap and molding, it is necessary to drill pilot holes in the pieces so the wood will not split when the nails are driven in. The holes should be made with a 5⁄64" (1.9mm) drill bit: one in the middle and two on each side. Apply T-88 glue to the surface of the top of the sign. Be sure to center the cap on the sign using the centering marks you drew earlier. Place the #16 1¼" (32mm) brads into the predrilled holes. After hammering the nails, use a nail set to drive them in about ⅛" (3mm). We will fill the holes later. Turn the sign on its cap, position the molding, and place the brads in the predrilled holes. Hammer in as before and drive them in below the surface with the nail set. The sign is now ready for filling, sanding, and priming.

**4 Fill the nail holes and voids.** There are many wood fillers on the market. Be sure to use one formulated for exterior use. I find Qwikwood, a two part exterior epoxy manufactured by Polymeric Systems, Inc., to be easy to use, quick drying, and versatile. It is readily available at most home improvement stores or online at *www.polymericsystems.com*. Be sure to read the safety instructions before use. Slice a ⅛"-¼" (3mm-6mm) wafer from the roll of epoxy—do not tear it, as you may not get the correct amount of hardener—and knead until the two parts are mixed. After filling any cracks, gaps and nail holes, use a little water to smooth. Let dry and sand to finish.

**5 Prime the sign.** Prime as described in Chapter 1 (page 27).

## BASECOAT THE SIGN

Most people have a hard time choosing colors. When selecting a background color, it's a good idea to consider the colors on the house. For example, you don't want to paint a sign dark brown if it's going to be hung on a dark brown house; tan or cream would be better choices. I want to use a dark red color for the background, because the house it will go on is a grayish tan and the trim is dark red. If I highlight the fruit enough, they will pop off the dark red. A number of alternate colors would work as well—white, off-white, dark green, and black, to name a few.

Also, take note of the colors that will appear in the artwork. The colors to be used in the artwork are green for the leaves, tan for the pineapple, yellow for the lemon, orange for the orange, purple for the grapes, and red and yellows for the peach and apples.

### PAINT COLORS

**California latex colors:**

- Colony red
- Nu-white
- Yellow: Special mix (Formula T-12y, used in Chapter 2)
- Black
- Tan: Special mix (Formula E-12, F-32, I-44, T-11y12)
- Crimson red
- Blue: Special mix (Formula B-3y24, E-6y24, D-12, Kx-42, V2y12)

**One Shot sign painter's enamels:**

- Letter white
- Chrome yellow
- Bright red

**1 Apply the background paint.** Here is the sign with three coats of primer followed by three coats of colony red. Be sure to paint the background color up on the edge of the molding—this will make painting the accent color on the molding neater. It would be very difficult to try to paint this edge another color without hitting the red background.

**2 Paint the molding and cap.** I have chosen a darker warm grayish tan for the molding and cap as an accent color. I used a soft round #10 sable to lay down a good coat of paint. After loading the brush, start at one end of the molding and pull along the edge in a steady straight line. After painting the molding, paint the cap and let dry. Two or three coats of paint will be needed for complete coverage.

**3** **Prepare to apply the basecoat to the fruit.** The next step is to basecoat the artwork-selecting the lighter tones of the various fruits. Since the base coat aspect of painting was discussed in detail in Chapters 1 and 2 (pages 29 and 46), I will give only a brief outline of the process here. Gather the following paint colors: white, yellow, black, tan, crimson red, and blue.

**4** **Paint the leaves.** Paint the leaves a light green made with 1 part black to 2 parts yellow and ½ part white.

**5** **Paint the pineapple.** Mix 1 part white to 1 part tan and paint the body of the pineapple.

**6** **Paint the lemon and peach.** Mix 1 part yellow to 1 part white to base-coat the top of the lemon and peach. Use straight yellow for the bottom half of each. Blend.

**7** **Paint the orange.** Use straight yellow for the top half of the orange, and a mix of 2 parts yellow and 1 part red for the bottom half, and blend.

**8** **Paint the apples.** Use straight yellow for the top of the apples and straight red for the bottoms and blend.

**9** **Paint the grapes.** Use 2 parts blue and 1 part red and 2 parts white to make a bluish purple for the grapes.

**10** **Touch up.** Due to the low hide nature of the yellow, you may want to repeat the painting of the peach, lemon, orange, and apples to achieve good coverage.

**The base coat is complete.**

## FINISH PAINTING THE ARTWORK

Note: Always have plenty of reference pictures of the items you are carving or painting. Books and greeting cards are a great source. Copying another artist was the traditional method of teaching in the days of the Renaissance and it still is a great way to learn. It is much easier than using a photo for a beginner. Copying someone else's work is fine—as long as you don't sell it. That's when copyright issues arise.

**1 Paint the leaves.** Using the same light green mixed for the basecoat (1 part black to 2 parts yellow and ½-part white), paint the outside edges of the leaf. Mix 1 part black to 1 part yellow for a dark green and paint the center portion of the leaf and blend. Highlight by tapping a touch of white near the top of the leaf in the light green area and blend slightly, taking care not to over blend. The highlight will disappear when you blend too much. Repeat these steps for the rest of the leaves.

Add the paint.

Blend the paint and add highlights.

**2 Paint the lemon.** Using a very light yellow, paint the top third of the lemon. Using straight yellow, paint the rest of the lemon, and blend well. Apply a small amount of white to the top of the lemon and blend slightly.

Add paint.

**3 Paint the apple.** Paint the top third of the apple with straight yellow and paint the rest crimson red. Blend well. Add a touch of white in the upper left of the yellow area and blend slightly. Repeat on the other apple.

Blend paint and add highlight.

**4 Paint the pineapple.** Paint a white area in the upper center of the pineapple. Using the tan color, paint the rest of the pineapple and blend well.

Apply yellow and red to upper peach.

**5** **Paint the orange.** Paint the top third of the orange with straight yellow. Mix 1 part yellow and 1½ parts red and paint the rest of the orange with this. Blend well. Add a touch of white to the upper left top of the orange and blend slightly.

**6** **Paint the peach.** Paint the top edge of the peach and the area to the upper right of the "scoop" with straight yellow, and the rest of the upper section with red. Blend.

Blend upper peach and add highlight.

Paint bottom of peach.

Blend and add crescent of red.

Completed peach.

Highlight with a touch of white on the top curve and blend slightly. Paint the top third of the lower section of the peach with white, and paint the rest with yellow. Blend the yellow and white well. Add a touch of red to the bottom crescent of the peach and blend.

**7** **Paint the grapes.** Begin by painting two or three grapes with the same light bluish purple and add a touch of white to the upper left. Blend slightly while both paints are still wet. Continue in the same manner until all the grapes are painted. Don't paint too many grapes at one time—they will dry before you can blend in the white highlight.

**8** **Detail the leaves.** Add some white to the light green mix for the leaves to make a light celery color. Mix the paint with a little water so it will flow well. The paint mixture should be of a creamy consistency, not a watery one. See the tip (below) for instructions on loading the script liner. With the script liner properly loaded, paint the thin vein lines down the center of the leaves.

### Loading a Script Liner

A properly loaded script liner will give you the ability to paint thin long lines. After mixing the correct color, add a little water to get a creamy consistency. To load the brush, put the brush in the paint up to the ferrule and wiggle it back and forth in the paint. Flip the brush over and repeat. Now you have a brush with a sharp chiseled edge, ready to use.

Wiggle the brush in the paint.

Top view.

Side view.

9 **Add deeper tones to the lemon.** Add the golden shadow color. Now, go over the individual fruits, adding the deeper shadows to each that will create the illusion of depth and roundness. Remember that, in general, lighter tones will bring the objects forward, and darker tones will push them back. Mix 1 part yellow with 1½ parts tan and a touch of red to make a golden color. Use this color to paint the lower right corner of the lemon. Dip your blender into some water; pat most of it off on a paper towel or paint rag. Use this damp brush to blend the golden shadow color into the rest of the lemon.

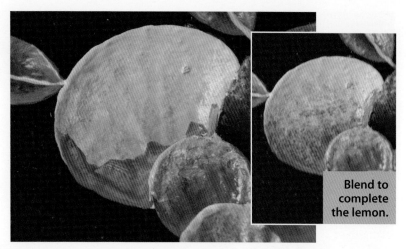

Blend to complete the lemon.

10 **Add deeper tones to the orange.** Mix more red into the color you made for the lemon to make a darker brownish orange. Paint this color on the bottom right of the orange. Blend as above.

Paint the bottom right.

Blend.

Add dark red.

Blend.

11 **Add darker tones to the apples.** Mix 1 part red with 1 part black to create a very dark red color. Use this color to paint the left hand area of the apple on the right, and blend with the dampened brush as above. Paint the right lower area of the apple on the left with the same dark red mix and blend.

Paint the bottom of the peach with dark red.

Add dark red to the split and blend.

**12** **Add darker tones to the peach.** Using the same dark red, paint the bottom of the peach, as shown. Blend the dark red at the bottom of the peach with a damp blender brush, and then add the dark red to the split in the peach and blend this as well.

Add brown.

Blend.

**13** **Detail the pineapple.** Mix 2 parts tan to 1 part red and 1 part black to make a dark brown. You may have to tweak this color mixture a bit—add more red if the color has a greenish tinge, more black if it appears too red. We will use this to add a shadow to each of the diamond-shaped elements of the pineapple. Paint the bottom of the diamond with the dark brown and blend with the damp blending brush.

Add dark purple to the right side of each grape.

Blend.

14 **Detail the grapes.** Using 2 parts blue and 1 part red, mix a dark bluish purple. Paint this in the lower right side of a grape and blend with a damp brush. Repeat for each grape. Use a touch of white to add a glint to the upper left of each grape.

Add white highlights.

15 **Paint the letters.** I will use One Shot lettering enamel again to paint the letters. Use a mix of a lighter tone put on the cap and molding for the letters. Mix 2 parts white to 1 part black, with ½-part yellow and ½-part red. Paint letters as explained on page 31. That completes the sign.

Here's the finished sign.

# CHAPTER 4:
# NOAH'S ARK

Sweet Dreams

oah's Ark is a cute piece for a baby or toddler. In addition to being used on a wall or door, it could be modified and used on a toy box or as a lamp base as well. Whenever I have a project that will be definitely used indoors, and is designed with small, delicate elements, such as this, I always choose basswood. It is more dense and even-grained than pine, so it doesn't fracture and split as readily and is much stronger. It is a favorite of those who carve in-the-round because of its ability to maintain its strength—it won't easily break even when carved very thinly. This is a great help when carving feathers, horns, fingers, etc. The color of the wood is a creamy tan—which makes painting with colored stains much easier than with a darker-toned wood.

For this carving, you'll need a piece of basswood 10" wide by 14" long by 1¾" thick (254mm x 356mm x 44mm). When tracing the pattern on the blank, be sure not to trace the zebra and the giraffe—they will be carved separately and added later.

## NEW TOPICS IN THIS CHAPTER

> Carving a simple banner

> Using a different type of wood— in this case, basswood

> Using a Dremel (power carver) to shape and texture

> Painting a finish with traditional artists' oil paints

## MATERIALS & TOOLS

- Piece of basswood, 10" wide by 14" long by 1¾" thick (254mm x 356mm x 44mm)
- Pattern
- Tape
- Pencil
- Ruler
- Carbon paper
- C-clamp
- Super glue for wood
- Chisels: 12mm skew, #2 8mm, #3 3mm, #3 12mm, #3 14mm fishtail, #3 25mm, #5 8mm, #5 12mm, #7 14mm, #9 15mm, #11 5mm, #15 6mm
- Assorted artist brushes—rounds, flats, and blenders
- Artists' oil paints—see painting section for list
- Band saw
- Sand paper
- Dremel rotary tool
- Bits for Dremel: ¼" (6mm) typhoon, ¼" (6mm) round ruby bit, ¼" (6mm) round fine diamond bit, ⅛" (3mm) round ruby bit, ¼" (6mm) round fine diamond bit

**Sweet Dreams Text for Banner**
Photocopy at 100%.

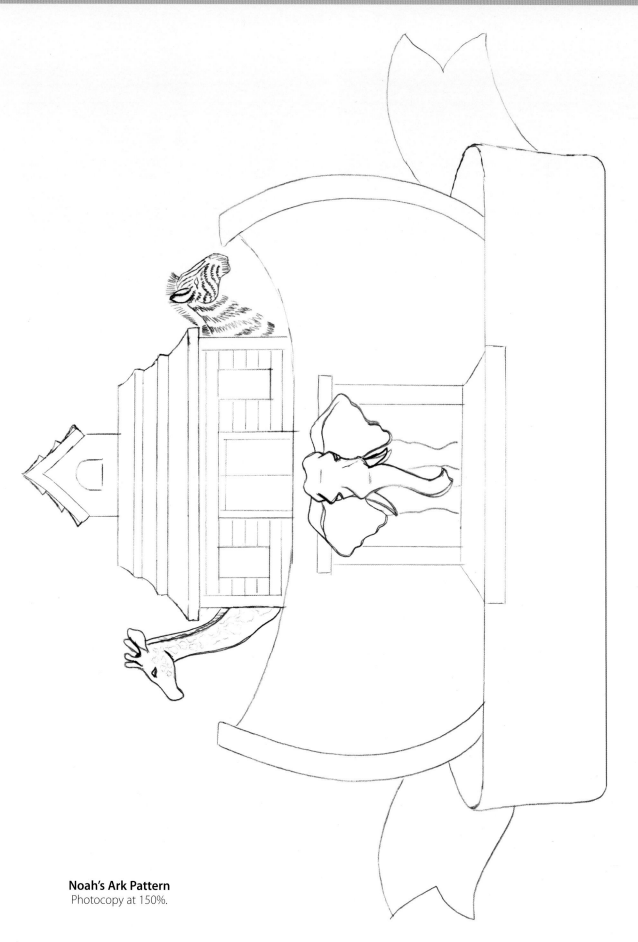

**Noah's Ark Pattern**
Photocopy at 150%.

## CUT OUT THE SIGN

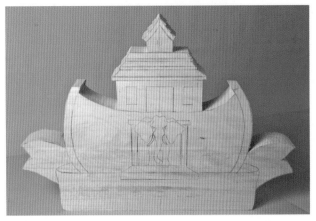

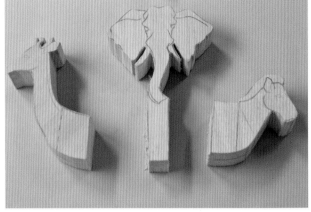

**1 Cut out the ark.** Transfer the pattern to the wood. Use a band saw to cut it out. Here is the ark after being cut out on the band saw. As we begin carving each element of the ark, we will be making depth markings on the sides of the carving. Unless otherwise stated, the measurement is from the top surface of the carving. These marks will help you stay on track and keep the guesswork out of creating this piece.

**2 Cut out the animal heads.** Using the extra pieces of basswood, trace and cut the animal heads (giraffe, elephant, and zebra). I recommend leaving on extra wood to serve as handles to make holding and clamping easier. They will be removed when the carving is complete. Note the direction the grain should be running—it should be as parallel to the thinnest parts of the piece as possible, such as the tusks and trunk of the elephant and the ears on the giraffe. This will give the potentially weakest parts of the structure the most support. Using the band saw, carefully cut the thickness of the animal heads so they will be at ¾" (19mm) thick, or simply use wood ¾" (19mm) thick.

## CARVE THE BANNER

Remember, as always, to clamp your work down before starting to carve. Banners are carved using a combination of rounded edges for the bend in the banner and scooped areas to create the illusion of the turn or fold.

**1 Mark the thickness.** Draw lines 1" (25mm) down from the surface at the top curve of the banner as shown.

**2 Carve down the banner.** Use the #15 6mm V-groove to cut the side of the ark where it meets the banner. Using a #7 14mm chisel, scoop the banner down to the 1" (25mm) line. This is an easy way to remove a larger amount of wood from an area. Next, stop-cut the line separating the lower banner with a #15 6mm V-groove and flatten this section of the banner to the depth mark with a #3 14mm fishtail. Repeat this on the banner end on the right.

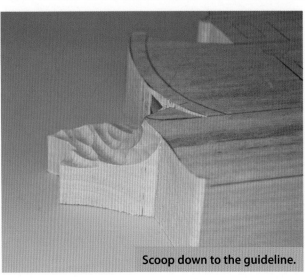

Scoop down to the guideline.

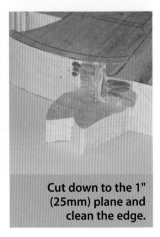

Cut down to the 1" (25mm) plane and clean the edge.

Top view.

3 **Lower the ends.** Scoop out a depression from top to bottom across the banner end near the pointed ends using the #9 15mm gouge. Blend the edges of the scooped depression to create a soft rolled edge.

4 **Roll the lower banner into the side.** Stop-cut the separation between the upper and lower portion of the banner with the V-groove and round the lower banner edge down into the cut about ¼" (6mm) as shown.

5 **Round the edge of the top banner.**

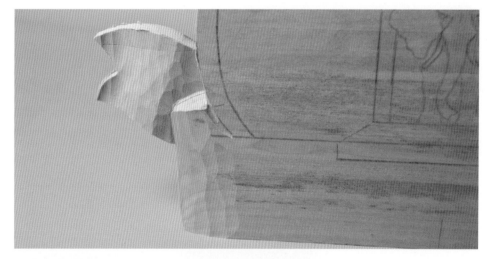

6 **Carve the curve of the top banner.** Draw the curve of the banner. Stop-cut the edge of the banner where it meets the ark. Using a #3 14mm fishtail, bevel the curve. Continue to re-cut the stop cut as needed to bevel the angle deeper. With a #7 14mm, carve a scoop in the angled curve. Repeat on the other side of the banner.

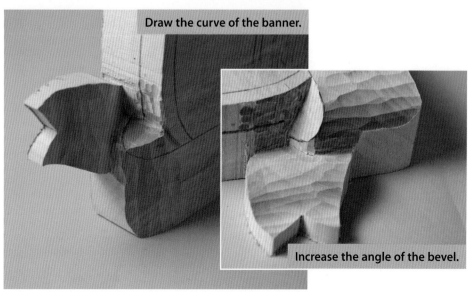

Draw the curve of the banner.

Increase the angle of the bevel.

## CARVE THE ARK

This ark is designed to be a high-sided round and fanciful little piece.

We will be doing some planking and other little details as we go.

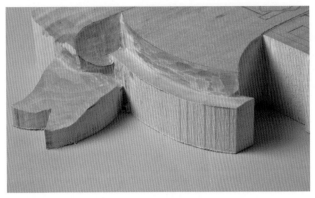

**1 Carve the keel.** Begin by marking the side of the keel about ¾"–1" (19mm–25mm) down—it should be just above the bottom of the scoop of the banner. We want the banner to look like it wraps around the keel. As before, first gouge the keel with a #9 15mm. Use the #15 6mm V-groove and the #3 14mm fishtail to square off the cut on the keel.

**2 Lower the wall surface.** Stop-cut the top and bottom of the wall portion of the first floor of the building on the ark to separate it from the ark and the roof. Using the #14mm fishtail, carve it down ⅛" (3mm) and redraw the windows, trim, door, and clapboards.

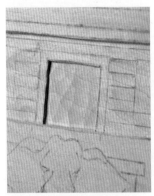

**Stop-cut the top edge of each board.**

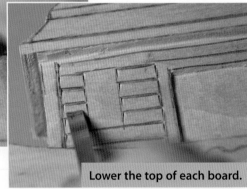

**Lower the top of each board.**

**3 Carve the inner door.** Stop-cut the inner edges of the door using the #15 6mm V-groove. Use your skew to cut the corners, and drop the surface ¹⁄₁₆" (1.6mm) with a #3 14mm fishtail.

**4 Carve the clapboard.** Using the 12mm skew, make a stop cut on both the right and left sides of each clapboard. Make the cut deeper at the top of each board. Now, stop-cut the top horizontal edge of each clap board. With a #2 8mm chisel, bevel each board so they are lower at the top.

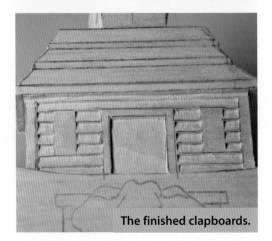

**The finished clapboards.**

5 **Rough-out the roof.** Stop-cut the roof of the first floor and drop the top story of the house ½" (13mm). Bevel the roof of the first floor down ⅜" (10mm) so the top of it is ⅛" (3mm) above the top story. Draw in the shingle edge and trim for the top story's roof and lower the wall portion of the top story ¹⁄₁₆" (1.6mm). Bevel the trim on the top story. Draw in the shingles on the first story's roof. Stop-cut the shingle top with the #15 6mm V-groove. Bevel the shingle top down into the stop cut. Repeat for the rest of the shingles.

Carve down the top story.

Bevel the trim on the top roof.

Stop-cut the shingle tops.

6 **Carve clapboards on the top story.** Draw in the details on the top story. Carve the clapboards as before.

7 **Continue carving the main roof.** Draw the ridge line on the roof and the separate shingles. Bevel the top shingle slightly under the ridge line. Now V-gouge the lines separating the shingles.

**8 Round the hull.** Stop-cut to separate the banner from the ark. Round the hull of the ark, stop-cutting the door frame and texturing the entire hull. Note that the stop cut has removed the top part of the elephant's head that extended over the door frame. Also note how the top of the banner is beveled down to the boat hull. Note how the banner wraps down and around the boat keel and hull, and the banner ends are below that.

Stop-cut between the banner and ark.

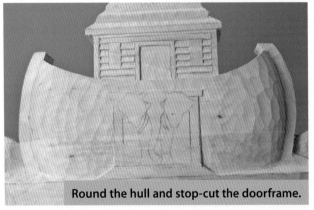

Round the hull and stop-cut the doorframe.

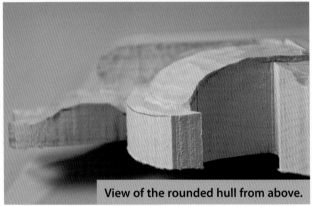

View of the rounded hull from above.

**9 Draw on the rail and planks.** Draw in the top rail of the ark so it is in line with the top of the door frame. The planks on the boat will be ¼" (6mm) wide, so begin marking ¼" (6mm) lengths next to the door frame, keel, and in the center of the spans. Draw in the planks.

## 10 Carve the planks.

Stop cut the right and left sides of the planking where it meets the door frame and keel with the 12mm skew. Make the cut deeper at the top of the plank edge, as was done for the clapboards. Stop-cut the top edge of each plank. Begin beveling the top of each plank lower. Due to grain direction, you will need to slice the first few planks with a #3 3mm. Continue slicing in this way, cleaning the edges with the skew. At the fourth row, where the grain flattens out, switch to a #3 14mm fishtail and bevel the edges as before on the clapboards.

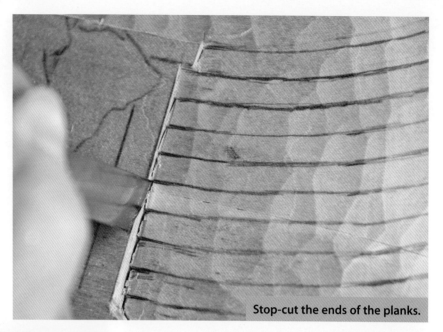

Stop-cut the ends of the planks.

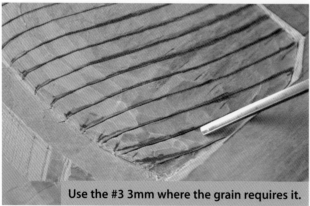

Use the #3 3mm where the grain requires it.

Bevel the edges of the planks.

Switch to a fishtail.

Beveling of planks finished.

**11** **Separate the planks.** Draw on the separations between planking boards and stop-cut them with the #15 6mm V-groove.

**Make sure the edges are clean.**

**12** **Clean up the edges.** Begin cleaning and texturing the edges of the carving with #3 14mm fishtail. This texturing is important. If the surface is not uniform, it will show in the painting and look messy. When carving an edge, be sure to carve the very edge from the back—this will prevent splitting off chunks of wood.

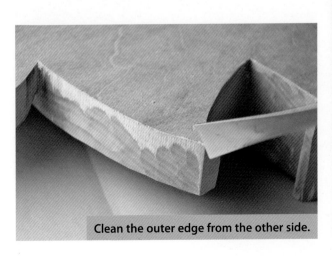

**Clean the outer edge from the other side.**

**Completed, cleanly carved edges.**

**13** **Undercut the banner ends.** Bevel the back edge of the banner slightly to give it a paper-thin appearance from the front. This is called undercutting, and is a method used to give the appearance of added dimension. Draw a line at ¼" (6mm) in from the edge on the back side of the banner ends, and stop cut the center *V* in the banner. Be sure to stop cut the base of the banner ends. Bevel the edge from the line drawn to the front edge of the banner. Bevel the bottom of the banner end. Repeat on the other edge of the banner and round the bottom of the banner from the back side.

Undercut to the *V* you drew.

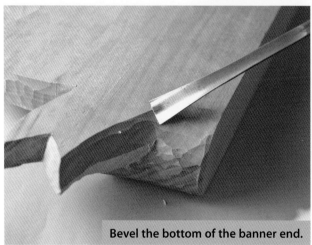

Bevel the bottom of the banner end.

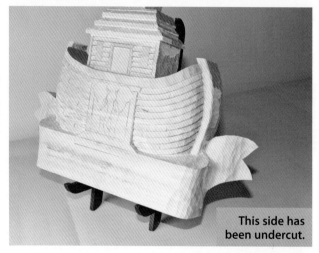

This side has been undercut.

This side has not been undercut.

The ark and house are finished.

## CARVE THE ELEPHANT HEAD

In any carving you undertake, the importance of collecting reference pictures or photos should never be overlooked. Every artist or craftsman depends on reference material to constantly refer to throughout the creation of the work. Before you undertake the carving of the elephant, be sure to gather some good photographs of elephants to refer to.

**1** **Work on the ears.** Begin the carving by stop cutting and dropping the ear ½" (13mm) from the surface. Draw in the top rims of the ears. Round over the tops of the ears. With a #11 5mm, scoop out a depression below the drawn line. Continue scooping out the lower portion of the ear to give it the wavy effect shown.

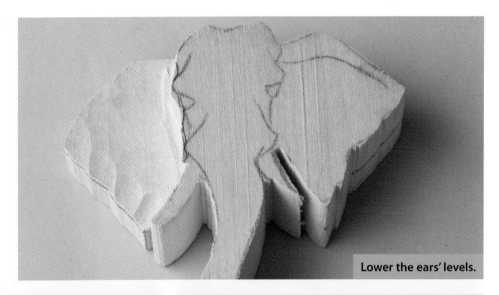
Lower the ears' levels.

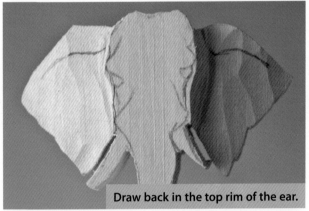
Draw back in the top rim of the ear.

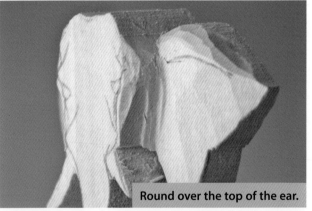
Round over the top of the ear.

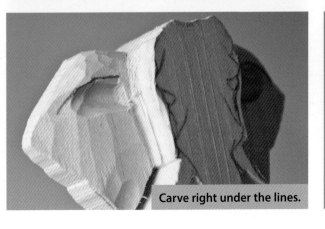
Carve right under the lines.

Scoop out the rest of the ear.

**2** **Slant the face.** The head slants back toward the forehead from a spot just below the tusks. Bevel from this point down ⅛" (3mm) to the top of the head. Redraw the facial features. Mark the point on the head indicated and round over the top of the head.

Carve the angle.

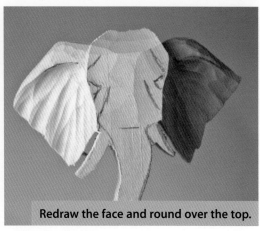

Redraw the face and round over the top.

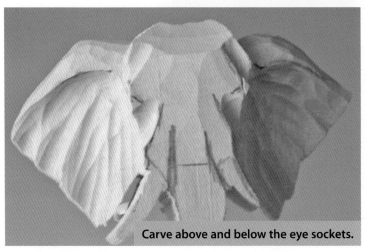

Carve above and below the eye sockets.

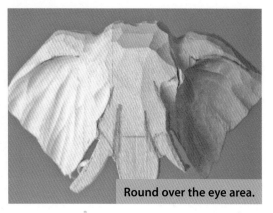

Round over the eye area.

**3** **Carve the eye areas.** Using the #11 5mm, scoop out depressions above the eye sockets and between the eyes and the tusks as shown. Round over the eye area.

**4** **Shape the tusks and trunk.** Draw a line on the side of the tusk as shown. Use the #11 5mm to scoop out wood along the line. Repeat on other tusk. Round over the tusks, and begin rounding the trunk.

Draw a line on the tusk side.

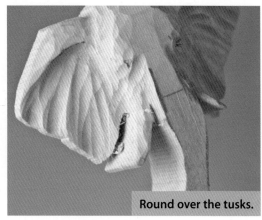

Round over the tusks.

5 **Work on the back of the head and ears.** Round over the top of the head and ears from the back of the piece. From the back, bevel the ear edges right up to the carved edge in the front.

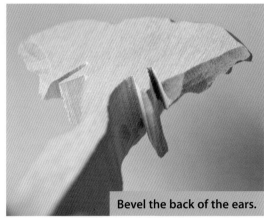

Bevel the back of the ears.

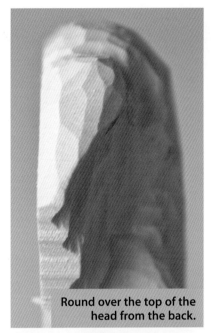

Round over the top of the head from the back.

6 **Continue shaping the trunk.** Draw on the shape of the trunk on the side as shown and remove the material behind the curve of the trunk with a #9 15mm. Remove the extra material behind the rest of the trunk, bracing it on scrap wood. Remove the wood in front of the trunk using a #5 8mm chisel. Cut the extra material from the bottom of the trunk. Draw the curve of the trunk from the front view. Remove the extra wood from around the trunk. Round the lower portion of the trunk. Cut a V in the bottom of the trunk.

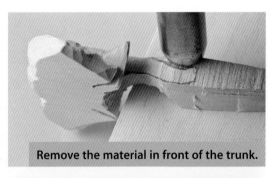

Remove the material in front of the trunk.

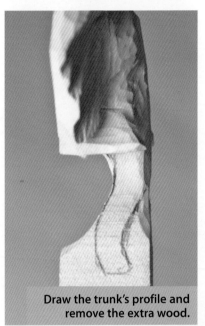

Draw the trunk's profile and remove the extra wood.

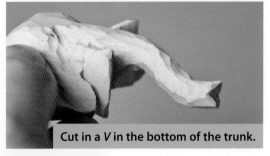

Cut in a V in the bottom of the trunk.

7 **Carve around the elephant.** Place the elephant head on the ark and draw around it. Stop-cut around the edges of the areas to both sides of the elephant and between its legs and drop them ¼" (6mm). Round-over the legs, gouging a path between the top of the leg and chest. Round the chest. Use a V-groove to stop-cut around the ramp to separate it from the banner.

8 **Texture the banner and ramp.** Texture the banner with a #3 25mm to match the texture on the curved portion of the banner, cutting around the ramp. Texture the ramp in the same way, leaving the edge above the banner. Give a slight tilt back to the top surface of the ramp toward the elephant's feet.

9 **Thin the tusks.** Now we will thin the tusks of the elephant. First, drip some super glue onto both tusks. This will fill the pores of the wood and add strength to the thin tusks. Carve the tusks so they are the same width on the sides as they are from the front, since they are round. You will be using a #11 5mm and a #5 8mm. You've completed the carving of the elephant. Do not attach it to the ark—it is easier and neater to paint it separately and assemble at the end.

## CARVE THE GIRAFFE

The giraffe is a side profile, as opposed to the front view of the elephant. In order to get the best effect for the ark, the heads of the giraffe and zebra will be carved in the round.

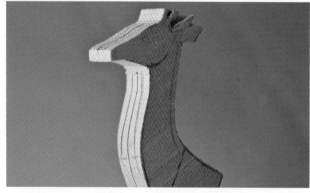

**TIP**

### Center Guideline

Whenever carving in the round, always start with a centerline and replace it if it is removed in the carving process. The centerline serves to keep you on track and prevents a lopsided carving.

1 **Draw in a centerline and front view.** Draw in the line down the center of the carving as well as a rough front view. This will show you what material you can remove in order to rough out the piece. Orient the grain direction so it runs in line with the horny growths. Draw in the centerline on the back of the giraffe as well.

2 **Rough-out the neck.** Use a #11 5mm to gouge under the jaw on both sides of the head. With a # 3 12mm, remove the extra material on both sides of the neck.

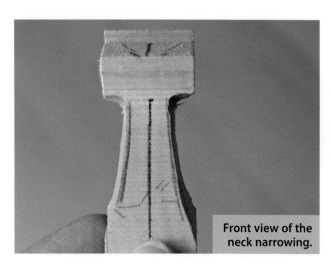

Front view of the neck narrowing.

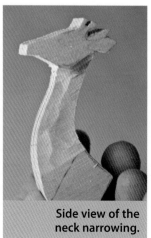

Side view of the neck narrowing.

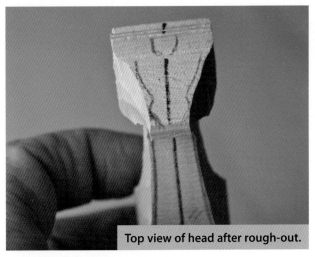

Top view of head after rough-out.

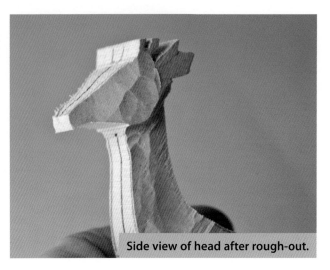

Side view of head after rough-out.

**3** **Rough-out the head.** Remove the extra material on the face of the giraffe.

The original surface on the right; the dropped surface on the left.

Remove the wood in the X areas.

**4** **Shape the ears.** Stop-cut and drop the right ear down ⅝" (16mm) from the original surface. Scoop out and remove areas marked with an *X* (to the outside of the ears and between them), cutting right through the carving. You will use a #11 5mm to gouge around the ear and a #5 8mm to shape it. From the back of the giraffe, stop-cut and drop the left ear ⅝" (16mm) down from the surface.

# POWER CARVE WITH A DREMEL ROTARY TOOL

From this point, we will use a different method to carve, called power carving, which is useful for easily and safely carving small details and pieces, as well as creating various textures such as hair, fur, or feathers. Pictured is a variable speed model 3001 Dremel. A variable speed gives you more versatility in carving and texturing. Always follow the safety precautions outlined in the manual. Use a dust mask or dust collecting system as well as safety goggles.

## CUTTING BITS

There is a variety of cutting bits, from coarse to fine. I will highlight here the types I have found useful. As you will note, they are mainly round bits in a variety of sizes, and also some cylindrical bits that are useful in texturing.

**Rough-out or coarse cutting bits:** Coarse cutting bit are aggressive and remove large amounts of material. There are several excellent brands, but the ones I prefer are called "Typhoon Rough-Out Burrs" and come in three color-coded grits—blue for the finest, red for medium, and black for coarse. I find the red to be the most useful. I like these because they don't have a tendency to become loaded or clogged up with wood like others I have used.

Pictured here is a ¼" (6mm) round red Typhoon bit. Notice how deeply it sits in the tool—this is for two reasons. You will have more control if the bit is close to your fingertips, as you do when using a pencil or a chisel. Also, if the bit is too far out of the tool's collet nut or chuck, it will wobble, making the shaft bent and unusable.

**Medium-grit bits:** Typically, ruby bits are the next type of bit you'd use for the stage when you're still shaping, but removing much less massive amounts of wood than during the roughing-out. They are available in three grits—super coarse, coarse, and regular. Again, although they are available in a variety of shapes, a selection of round bits in different sizes are most useful. You may also want 1 or 2 cylindrical bits for adding textures.

**Fine-grit bits:** The finest bits I use are diamond bits, and they come in fine and regular grits. Like the rubies, they are available in many shapes, but the round in a variety of sizes with some cylindrical in different sizes are the ones you will use most of the time.

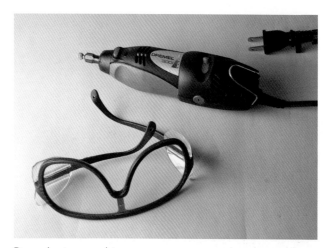

Dremel rotary machine.

¼" (6mm) round red Typhoon bit, properly seated deep in the tool shaft.

1 **Mark and shape the ears and neck.** Draw the gouge line around the base of the ear. Use the rotary tool with a ¼" (6mm) round red Typhoon bit to round the neck of the giraffe and to cut the gouge under the ears. Continue rounding the entire neck.

Remove wood at the base of the ears.

Round the neck.

2 **Round over the sharp edges.** Round over the sharp edges of the face—it will start to look like a giraffe soon. Round the back of the ears. Note the top of the nose is rounded while the bottom is left flat.

Shape the face of the giraffe.

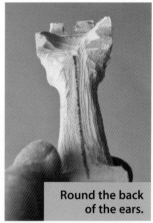

Round the back of the ears.

3 **Perform final shaping.** Change the bit to a ⅛" (3mm) regular ruby. Round the knobs on the top of the head and slant the ears down to blend into the head. Scoop out a depression in the ear and smooth the body and head with the ruby bit. Switch to a ⅛" (3mm) fine diamond bit and smooth the head, neck, ears, and knobs of the giraffe. Finish the giraffe by sanding lightly.

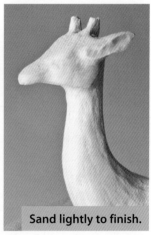

Sand lightly to finish.

Round the knobs and slant the ears.

# CARVE THE ZEBRA

The zebra should be somewhat easier to carve, in that it doesn't have knobs like the giraffe. Remember to gather your reference materials. We will be adding a fur texture to the mane, which is a simple but very attractive and realistic touch. We will use the Dremel for this.

**1** **Mark up the zebra.** Draw the centerline on the zebra as well as the front view. Note the direction of the wood grain. Draw the centerline on the back of the head as well as the two lines ⅛" (3mm) to either side of the center. These are the edges of the mane.

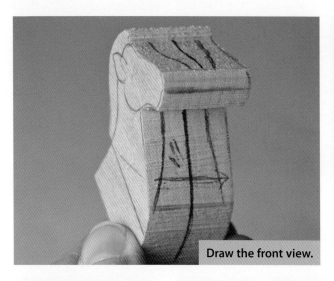

Draw the front view.

Draw on the edges of the mane.

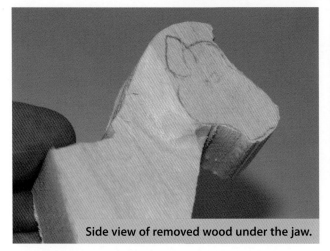

Side view of removed wood under the jaw.

Remove the wood on the top of the head, outside the mane.

**2** **Rough-out the zebra head.** Gouge under the jaw of the zebra, and remove the extra material on the neck. Remove the extra material on the top of the head on either side of the mane with a #11 5mm chisel. Remove the extra wood on the sides of the face. Using the ¼" (6mm) typhoon red round bit in the Dremel, remove the material on either side of the mane.

Remove the wood on the outside of the mane.

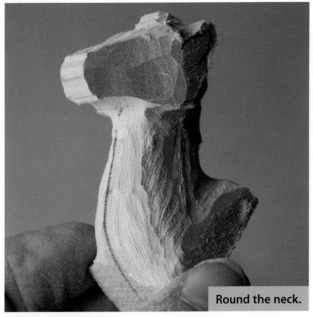

Round the neck.

Make a depression under the ear.

Bevel the ears.

3 **Refine the zebra.** Round the neck of the zebra with the Dremel. Make a depression under the ear. With the same bit, round the face of the zebra slightly and cut around the ear, leaving it high. Bevel the ears so they blend into the head at their bases.

4 **Detail the zebra.** Switch to the ⅛" (3mm) ruby bit and smooth the head. Also scoop out the center of the ears. Smooth the zebra with the ⅛" (3mm) diamond bit. Switch to a ⅛" (3mm) diamond cylindrical bit. Use the bit to cut in the texture on the mane.

5 **Mark the position of the two heads.** Clamp the giraffe head to the back of the ark and draw the line on the giraffe where it meets the edge of the house. This is where the giraffe needs to be cut to fit onto the house after painting. Repeat for the zebra head.

**TIP**

**Texturing Hair**

It is a common belief that to create a hair texture, you need to use a bit with a pointed tip to "draw" on the hair lines. Actually, the only thing that happens is that the tip wanders all over the carving. The cylindrical bit shown is the best to use.

# STONING

At this point, you can choose to skip down to the painting section, or follow the optional instructions to "stone" or texture the fur of the giraffe and zebra given here. The stoning will be done using the Dremel, and will enhance the look of the giraffe and zebra.

As a general rule, fur growth on most animals starts at the nose and grows straight down the center of the skull and down the spine to the tail. On the sides and chin of the face, it will begin straight back at first, and then begin to gently curve around the eyes, up on the ears, and down the neck. It tends to flow over the skin, almost like water. There will never be a sharp or abrupt change of direction on the fur when the animal is in a standing position. For more realistic fur or hair texture, stagger the stoning marks so they don't begin or end in a line, and curve the marks slightly.

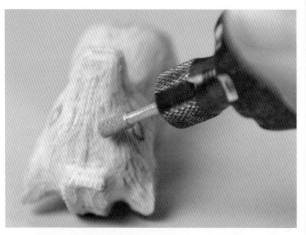

1 **Draw on fur guidelines.** First draw on some guidelines showing the direction of the fur. These lines will serve to keep you on track, and give a nice flow to the fur. Be sure to use your reference images while plotting the flow of the fur.

2 **Stone the head.** Using a cylindrical ⅛" (3mm) diamond bit, begin stoning from the nose down the top of the head in short strokes. Now repeat these steps for the giraffe—the elephant will not be stoned, since it has a skin texture, not fur.

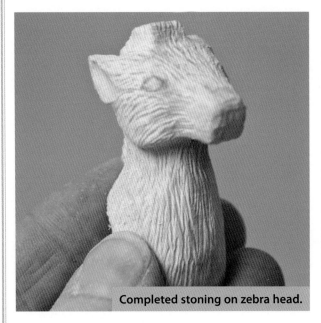

Completed stoning on zebra head.

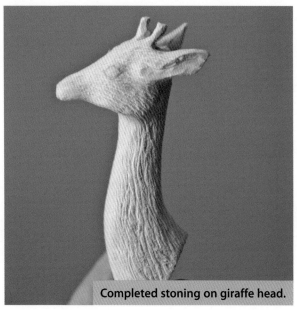

Completed stoning on giraffe head.

## PAINTING THE SIGN

Since this project is destined for interior use, the options for finishing are almost unlimited. You can choose to simply seal it with a finishing oil, urethane, or lacquer, or add some color with washes of acrylic or artists' oil paints. I prefer artists' oils, because the colors are usually richer and the long drying time allows the painter to relax, taking your time to blend colors. Beginning painters generally prefer this option.

I use Winton oil colors, manufactured by Winsor Newton. They are of good quality—smooth and finely ground, never grainy. They have a number system in addition to the color names, as well, which make quick identification easy.

## PAINT THE GIRAFFE

Apply paint.

**1** **Apply the basecoat.** To more easily hold the head while you paint, insert a thumbtack in the back of the neck and grab it with a clothespin. Equip your palette with a small amount (⅛" [3mm] long) of the following colors: white, yellow ochre, raw sienna, and burnt umber. Paint on some white, slightly thinned with thinner, on the cheek, chest, and ear edges. Paint some thinned yellow ochre on the rest of the giraffe. Blend well.

Blend.

## MATERIALS & TOOLS

- Paint thinner
- Paint cloths for cleaning brushes
- Palette (Either a prepared palette or a sheet of tin foil on a firm, thin board)
- Brushes—a variety of synthetic flats and rounds, as well as a script liner. You will also want some blenders, either synthetic or bristle. I usually have a few of each in different sizes available.

**Paint:**

- #2 Burnt sienna
- #3 Burnt umber
- #8 yellow
- #25 Lamp black
- #33 Prussian blue
- #34 Raw sienna
- #35 Raw umber
- #40 Titanium white
- #44 Yellow ochre

Note: All colors are thinned to make a wash unless otherwise stated.

**2** **Add raw sienna to the neck and jaw.** Paint a little raw sienna at the base of the neck and under the jaw and blend each area.

**3** **Add coloring to head.** Now, use the raw sienna to paint the area at the top of the head and the nose. Blend. Add some burnt umber to the nose, top of the head, and tips of the knobs; blend.

**4** **Add eyes.** Add a streak of raw sienna under the area where the eye will be and blend. Draw on both eyes with a pencil. Use the pattern for help. The eye should be almond-shaped and pointed toward the nose and the ear as shown. Try to have the eyes match in location on either side of the head. Looking down helps with front-to-back alignment. Looking face-on helps with the up-or-down placement. Use a script liner to paint in the eye with burnt umber. Add a white glint where shown.

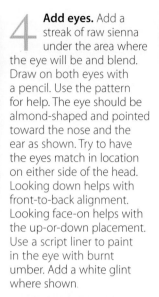

**5** **Paint the mane.** Add some burnt umber to the spine and blend slightly—this is the mane of the giraffe.

**6** **Paint the spots.** You may want to draw the spots on the giraffe. Refer to the pattern for help. As a rule, they are irregular in shape, beginning light and small, and getting larger and darker as you go down the neck. Notice that the area between the spots is a uniform width. Using just some raw sienna and a small round brush (#2 or 3), begin painting the spots on the giraffe, starting on the jaw under the eye. Next, mix 1½ parts raw sienna to 1 part burnt umber, and paint larger, darker spots on the top of the neck. Use a darker mix—more burnt umber—as you proceed down the neck, painting even larger spots.

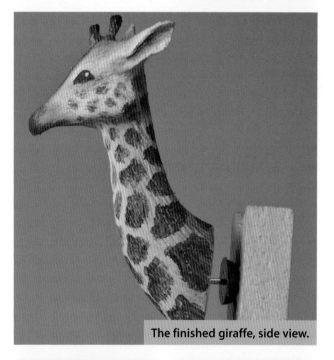

The finished giraffe, side view.

Front view of the finished giraffe.

Back view of the finished giraffe.

> **TIP**
>
> **Blending**
> When blending, if the paint seems a little dry, try adding some thinner—darker colors can always be blended with a little thinner.

## PAINT THE ZEBRA

We will be using the following colors for the zebra:
White, raw umber, raw sienna, yellow ochre, and black.
Notice in your references, that the white areas have some
shading as well as some yellow tones. Attention to these
details pushes your final product from good to great.

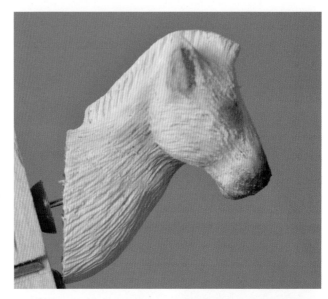

1 **Add dark markings.** Begin by painting the entire head of
the zebra with white paint that has been thinned to
a creamy consistency. Mix 1 part raw umber to 1½ parts
raw sienna. Paint this on the nose, eye area, inner ear, and
under the jaw. Blend and let dry. The next step will be to paint
on the black stripes; the white needs to be dry, or the two
colors will blend and make grey.

**Add yellow and draw on the stripes.**

**Left side view of the black stripes.**

**Front side view of the black stripes.**

**Right side view of the black stripes.**

2 **Add the stripes.** Wash on some yellow ochre near the
nose and front of the neck. Next, draw the black stripes
on the zebra. Mix 1 part black to 1 part raw umber and
paint on the stripes and the eye. With a mix of 4 parts raw
sienna and 1 part white, thin the mix slightly and paint in the
light tan stripes between the black ones using a script liner.

**Finished zebra.**

# PAINT THE ELEPHANT

Colors used for the elephant: white, raw umber, and raw sienna. The elephant is a gray, dusty guy with well-placed highlights that give him interest and dimension. This is a great example of the effect highlights and shadows can have.

**1** **Add shadows.** Begin by mixing two colors. First, mix the dark tone with 1 part raw umber to 1½ parts raw sienna. Take about half of this and mix 1½ parts white to it. This is the light tone. Paint a slightly thinned wash of the light tone on the elephant, leaving the back unpainted so it can be glued later. Add some of the darker mix to the lower shadowed areas shown on the ears and the head, and blend.

**2** **Add highlights.** Add some white to the forehead, top of the ears, and the high spots in the ears, and blend.

**3** **Add dark tone to the trunk.** Using the dark tone, add some paint to the bend in the trunk and the eye/tusk area and blend. Darken the underside of the trunk and blend.

Darken the eye areas and the bend in the trunk.

Darken the back of the trunk.

**4** **Add more highlights.** Add some white highlights to the trunk, above and below the bend, to make these areas appear higher. Paint the top portions of the tusks raw sienna, and the lower portions white. Blend both areas. Add some white to the area above the tusks and blend. Add white highlights to area above and in front of where eyes will go and blend.

**5** **Add eyes.** Draw on the eyes and paint them with raw umber. Put a white glint in the 2 o'clock position on both eyes. With a script liner, paint thin curvy lines of raw umber across the top of the trunk (stop when you reach the top white area).

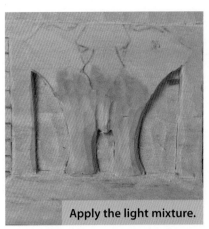

Apply the light mixture.

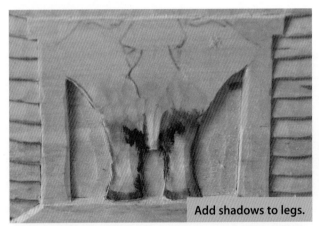

Add dark tone to the top and sides of the legs.

**6** **Paint the back of the ears.** With raw umber, paint the undercut area behind the ears.

**7** **Apply basecoat to the legs.** Now we will paint the legs of the elephant, which have been carved on the ark. Paint the legs with the light mixture you mixed in step 1. Paint the darker tone on the top and sides of the legs and blend.

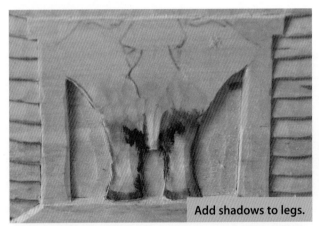

Add shadows to legs.

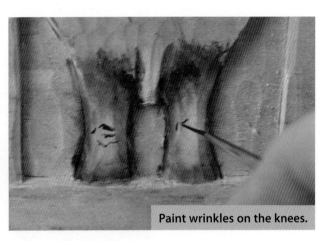

Paint wrinkles on the knees.

**8** **Add detail to legs.** Add some white highlights to the knees and blend. Add some raw umber shadows to the legs and blend. With a script liner, add raw umber wrinkles to the knees.

**9** **Paint the door opening.** Paint the area inside the door with raw umber (see photo 7 on page 98). Leave some of the area unpainted so the glue can adhere. Place—do not glue—the elephant head on its body to be sure all areas that can be seen are covered with raw umber. Set the head aside to dry while we paint the ark.

# PAINT THE ARK

Colors used: white, yellow, raw sienna, burnt sienna, burnt umber, Prussian blue, and black. Although this piece was designed for use in a child's room, we will use some softer shades that would be acceptable anywhere in the home. We will use a wood tone for the boat and roof, with a soft green house and a pretty blue banner. As in other paintings done in this book, be sure to follow all the shading steps—it will result in a fantastic project.

**1 Wash the ark.** Wash the boat part of the ark with thinned raw sienna. Include the keel and the deck top.

**2 Mark the positions of the heads.** Position the giraffe and zebra heads and draw a line around them on the house wall. Draw another smaller circle inside this one. We need to leave this area unpainted in order to glue the heads on later. Making the circle smaller ensures you will not see any raw wood when the heads are attached. I cut some circles the same size out of painter's tape to cover the area—then I don't have to worry that I might paint over them later.

**3 Wash the roof.** Wash the raw sienna over both roofs and the upper door, as well as the ramp.

**4 Paint the windows.** Paint white on the bottom halves of the windows and yellow on the upper halves. Blend. Paint on some burnt sienna, which is a reddish brown, in a rounded shape at the top of the window and blend. Be careful not get any burnt sienna near the white—you will get a pinkish color. Keep the yellow barrier color between them.

Blend burnt umber near the doorframe and the keels.

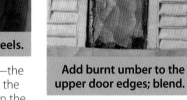

Add burnt umber to the upper door edges; blend.

5 **Add burnt umber detailing.** Begin shading the ark by dampening—not soaking—the boat with thinner. Paint some burnt umber next to the door and the keel. Blend so the border of the colors is soft, and also so some of the original raw sienna is retained in the middle of each half. After dampening the upper door with thinner, paint burnt umber on the edges of the door and blend.

Paint the deck.

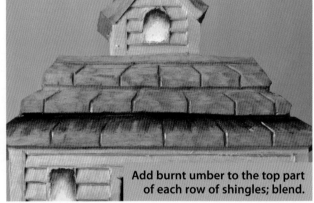

Add burnt umber to the top part of each row of shingles; blend.

6 **Paint the deck and shingle shadows.** Paint full-strength burnt umber on the top deck as shown, leaving a ⅛" (3mm) border around the edges. Paint burnt umber on the top of the row of shingles and blend downward. Repeat for all the roof shingles.

7 **Add highlights to ark.** Add some white to the top of the ark (between the doors), the top of the ramp under the elephant's feet, and the front edges of the shingles. Blend.

8 **Add detail to planking.** Use a toothpick dipped in burnt umber to add the nails to the boat planking. I suggest two nails on each plank end.

9 **Add detail to shingles.** Using a script liner loaded with thinned burnt umber, add lines separating the individual roof shingles.

10 **Detail the ramp.** Paint in the boards and splits in the ramp with the script liner. Use the toothpick with burnt umber to dot in the nails on the ramp.

11 **Detail the upper door.** With the same script liner, paint in the splits in the door on the house. Use black to paint on the hinges.

**Apply the light sage color.**

**Blend the dark olive next to the doors and windows.**

12 **Paint the house.** Mix 1 part black to 1 part yellow for a dark olive. Take some of this mix and mix 1 part of this dark mix to ½ part white. Give the house a coating of this light sage. Use the dark mix to paint the edges of the house next to the doors and windows, and blend. Use the light sage mix to paint the window and door trim. Use the darker color to paint the window panes.

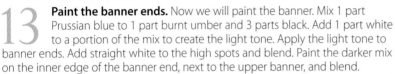

Add white highlights.

Paint the dark mix on the inner edge of the banner ends.

13 **Paint the banner ends.** Now we will paint the banner. Mix 1 part Prussian blue to 1 part burnt umber and 3 parts black. Add 1 part white to a portion of the mix to create the light tone. Apply the light tone to banner ends. Add straight white to the high spots and blend. Paint the darker mix on the inner edge of the banner end, next to the upper banner, and blend.

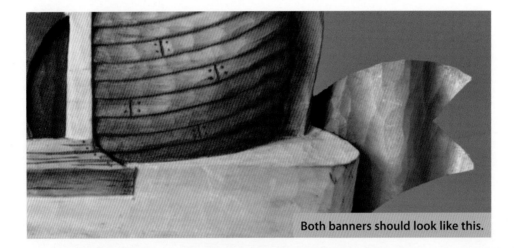

Both banners should look like this.

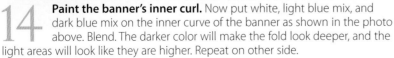

Apply the three colors.

Blend.

14 **Paint the banner's inner curl.** Now put white, light blue mix, and dark blue mix on the inner curve of the banner as shown in the photo above. Blend. The darker color will make the fold look deeper, and the light areas will look like they are higher. Repeat on other side.

**Paint the banner and shade under the ramp.**

**Add white highlights.**

**15** **Paint the banner.** Wash a slightly thinned light blue mixture over the top of the banner. Blend this into dark blue paint on the sides. Shade with dark blue under the ramp and blend. Add un-thinned white to the banner edges and blend.

**16** **Paint the lower door frame.** Paint the door trim around the elephant the light sage house color in the center, and the dark olive at the top and bottom, and blend.

**Adhere the elephant head.**

**All the animal heads are attached.**

**17** **Attach animal heads.** Glue on the elephant head. I use a product called Locktite, which is a super glue made for wood. Be sure it sits where you want it the first time—this glue instantly grabs and, unfortunately, there is no readjusting possible. Remove the painter's tape on the sides and glue on the other two heads. The ark can remain this way, but I chose to paint on "Sweet Dreams." Letters this small are very difficult to carve. You can scan the pattern of the banner into a computer and type in any name or phrase you like. Trace the print-out onto the banner with a dressmaker's carbon, which is chalk-based and will wash off when the letters are dry.

CHAPTER 5:

# IRISH CLADDAGH SIGN

A claddagh is a traditional Irish symbol of friendship or love. Sometimes worn as a ring or pendant, it features a heart for love, two hands for friendship, and a crown for loyalty. The phrase "Cead Mile Failte" is an Irish saying meaning "A hundred thousand welcomes," which makes a great greeting for a house sign.

# MATERIALS & TOOLS

- (1) Pine blank, 22" x 16" x 1¼" (559mm x 406mm x 32mm), for the background of the sign

- (1) Pine blank, 21" x 5½" x 1¼" (533mm x 140mm x 32mm), for the banner

- (1) Pine blank, 13" x 8½" x 1¼" (330mm x 216mm x 32mm), for the claddagh

- Printed pattern of claddah and banner with text

- Pencil

- Ruler

- Tape

- String

- Carbon paper

- Assorted chisels

- #16 brads

- Wire cutters

- Exterior epoxy (I use the System 3 T-88 mentioned earlier)

- Black medium grit smalt (a crushed black glass for the finish on sign)

- Latex primer

- Latex colors: Black, Putnam ivory, tan

- One Shot Signpainter's paint: enamel black, chrome yellow and dark green

- 23K Patent gold leaf

- Gold size

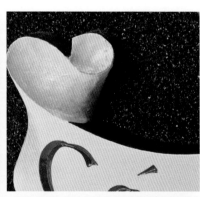

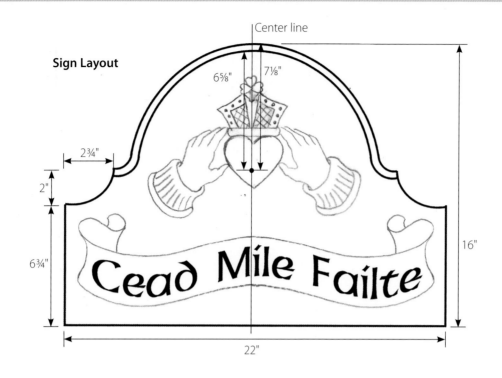

**Sign Layout**

Center line

6⅝"  7⅛"

2¾"

2"

6¾"

16"

22"

Center line

**Claddagh**
Photocopy at 200%.

**Banner**
Photocopy at 100%.

## LAY OUT THE SIGN SHAPE

1 **Draw the centerline.** Grab the piece of wood for the main sign. As always, on any shape that is symmetrical (the same shape on both sides), the first step is to draw the centerline from top to bottom.

2 **Measure and mark.** Now, on both the right and left side of the sign, measure up 6¾" (172mm) from the bottom and mark it. From that point, measure up 2" (51mm) and toward the center 2¾" (70mm) and mark that point. Next, measure down 7⅛" (181mm) from the top center and mark the spot. This is the radius point.

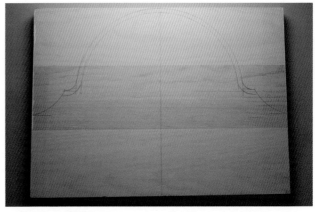

3 **Draw the arcs.** Using a string with a loop tied into the end, draw the arc in the manner described previously in Chapter 2 (page 36). Shorten the string ½" (13mm) and draw another arc inside the first. Draw curved shoulders as described on page 36, but make the shoulders concave, as you can see in the photo.

4 **Transfer the claddagh and banner patterns.** Transfer the designs for the claddagh and the banner to their respective blanks.

5 **Band saw the pieces.** Cut out all three pieces using the band saw.

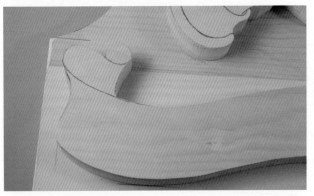

6 **Position the pieces.** Measure the background sign blank and mark 1" (25mm) up from the bottom, and in ¾" (19mm) from each side. Place the banner on these marks to locate it on the blank. Measure down 8" (203mm) from the center of the sign and mark. This is where the pointed bottom of the heart should be placed, lining up the center of the design to the centerline drawn. Trace around the banner and claddagh so you will know where to place them when they are done and ready to glue to the sign.

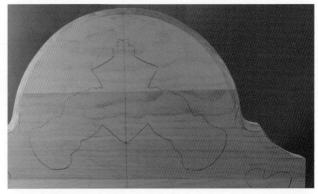

7 **Carve the bevel.** Draw bevel ½" (13mm) in from curved edge. Carve the bevel as described in Chapter 1 (page 25), using a #2 20mm chisel. Start at the top of the sign and carve in the direction of the arrows. Carve off the area between the outer curve and the inner curve you made earlier.

# CARVE THE BANNER

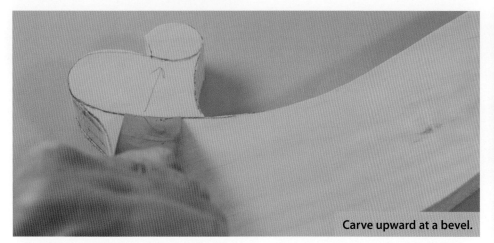

Carve upward at a bevel.

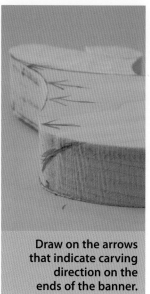

Draw on the arrows that indicate carving direction on the ends of the banner.

**1** **Mark and carve the curl.** Bevel top curl of banner down ½" (13mm) from banner edge where the chisel edge is located in the photo above. Bevel the curled area of the banner from the top drawn edge of the banner upward. There is no stop cut. Redraw the upper curl loop. Draw the arrows indicating the area of the banner edge to round, as well as the curve on the side to show the final shape. Use a #3 20mm chisel to round the edge of the banner. Label the small loop *B* and the large loop "A." Use a #7 14mm to scoop out the *A* curl of the banner. Follow up with a #11 4mm to cut closer to the edge and down around the edge of the *A* curl. Now scoop out the rest of curl "A." Using a #7 14mm, scoop out curl "B." Repeat on right side of banner.

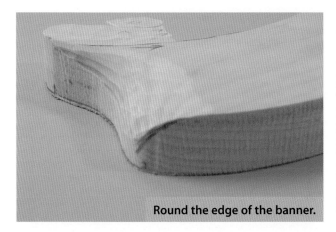

Round the edge of the banner.

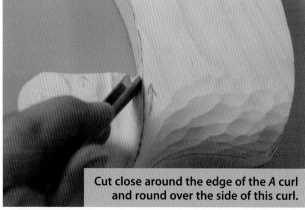

Cut close around the edge of the *A* curl and round over the side of this curl.

**2** **Transfer the letters to the banner.** Sand the carved curls on the banner and prepare to transfer the lettering by enlarging the pattern at the indicated percentage and cutting it out to fit the banner. Place on the carved banner and trace. Note the stop-cut lines. This font is called "Unical."

**3** **Carve the letters.** Carve the letters in the same way as outlined in Chapters 1 and 2.

## CARVE THE CLADDAGH

We will begin with the crown and shamrock, and then move on to the hands. I like to complete the outer elements in a design when possible and move on to the interior ones afterward.

Carve a groove above the crown band.

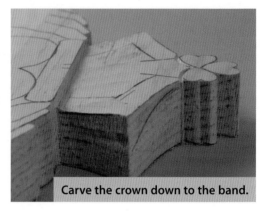

Carve the crown down to the band.

**1** **Bevel the crown surface.** Bevel the crown down ⅛" (3mm) from the top toward the band. Start by cutting a groove above the crown band that is ⅛" (3mm) deep.

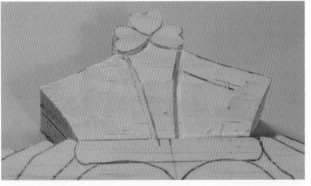

**2** **Carve the crown's stop cuts.** Make a V-groove stop cut on either side of the center detail and drop the area on either side ⅛" (3mm). Also make a stop cut under the shamrock at the top.

**3** **Create the crown's V.** Drop the surface of the center detail ¹⁄₁₆" (2mm) and draw a vertical line down the middle of it. Draw the elongated *V* in the center detail with the aid of the middle line. Stop-cut the center of the *V* and bevel the edges into the stop cut. You will have to stop-cut the upper edge of the *V* with a skew to separate it from the bottom of the shamrock.

**4** **Shape the crown.** Draw the curve on the top edge of the crown and separate the crown from the band with a stop cut. With a #3 14mm fishtail, round the edge of the crown in the direction of the arrows. Repeat on the other side.

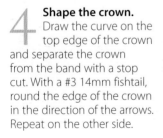

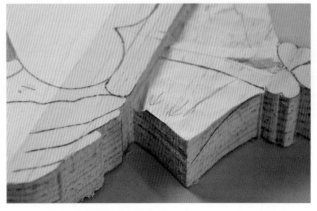

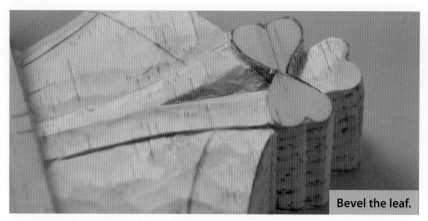

Bevel the leaf.

V-cut veins into the leaves and add centerlines to the crown's squares.

**5** **Carve the shamrock.** Draw the lines on the edge of the crown as shown. Stop-cut the top shamrock leaf. Bevel the leaf so it slopes toward the center. Bevel the other two leaves. Draw in the center veins and draw the lines that divide each half of the crown into quarters. V-cut the veins on each leaf and the lines drawn on the crown. Draw in the centerlines on the four squares, as shown. Bevel the leaf into the center stop cut. You may want to use the skew at the base of the leaf to clean it. Complete the other leaves of the shamrock in the same way.

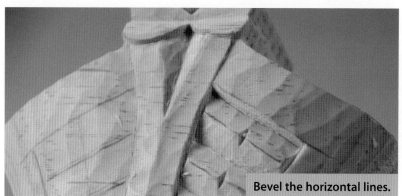

Bevel the horizontal lines.

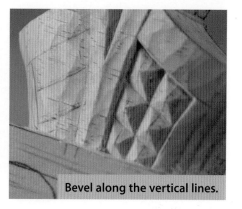

Bevel along the vertical lines.

**6** **Carve the crown detail.** The end goal of the texturing you're doing with the squares in the crown is to create a field of squares with four beveled triangular sides each, culminating in a point in the middle. Start by beveling the upper main horizontal line so that the main line is the low point, and the two smaller horizontal separations are the high points. Use a #2 8mm chisel. Repeat the bevel on the lower row, using the #2 5mm. Bevel the top edge. Redraw the vertical centerlines that divide each square into four. Bevel down to the left and right side from the vertical line drawn to the stop cut, leaving a raised pyramid shape. Continue to bevel the edges and clean the cuts as you go. When done, repeat on the other side.

**7** **Lower the area between the hands and the heart.**
Now lower the two areas between the hand and the heart down ⅜" (10mm). Begin by scooping out as much material as possible with the #11 4mm, and then use a variety of chisel shapes to stop-cut and clean as best you can. We will be able to finish later when we carve the hands and heart.

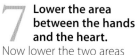

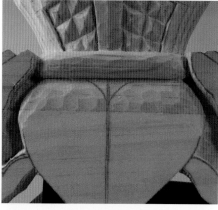

**8** **Shape the top of the heart and the crown band.** Round over the top of the heart and separate the band of the crown from the finger with a stop cut. Round the band edges to the left and right. Roll over the top and bottom edge of the band. Draw in the top of the heart shape.

## CARVE THE HANDS AND CUFFS

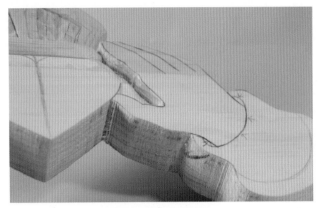

1 **Stop-cut to the left and right of the hand.** Stop-cut the two small lines separating the hand from the curve of the cuff on the left and right sides of the hand. Mark the line of the bevel.

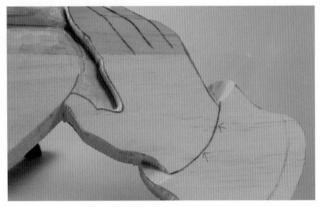

2 **Bevel the sides of the cuff.** Bevel the curved portion of the cuff to the line drawn on the side. Bevel around the hand on both sides.

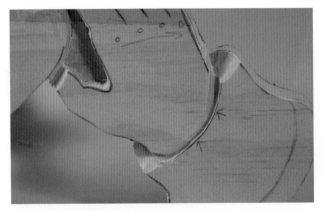

3 **Stop-cut the cuff.** Stop-cut the line indicated by the arrows on the cuff. Also, stop-cut the line between the thumb and heart. Draw in the knuckles, as shown.

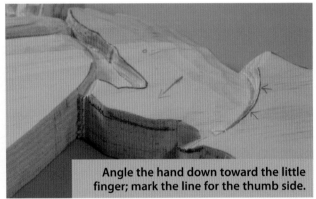

**Angle the hand down toward the little finger; mark the line for the thumb side.**

4 **Begin shaping the hand.** Draw a line ⅜" (10mm) down from the surface on the little finger side of the hand. Bevel the hand down to this line from the first knuckle. Slant the portion of the hand between the thumb and the cuff toward the cuff. Draw a line ¼" (6mm) down from the surface on the thumb side of the hand and bevel the thumb down to this line. Repeat on other hand. Round-over the thumb. Using a #11 7mm gouge, round-over the curve between the thumb and finger.

**The left hand is roughed-out; the right thumb has been smoothed.**

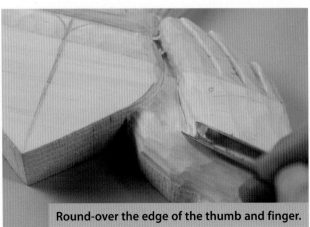

**Round-over the edge of the thumb and finger.**

## 5 Shape the fingers.
Redraw the lines separating the fingers and stop-cut them using a V-groove tool. Mark the joints of the fingers. Use your own hands as reference. Block out the angles of the fingers by increasing the beveling from joint to joint. From the first joint of the fingers, increase the bevel of all the fingers. Carve each finger so that the tip is lower than the first joint. Re-cut the stop cuts between the fingers to separate them. Begin to round each finger. Mark the knuckles again. Use the #11 7mm

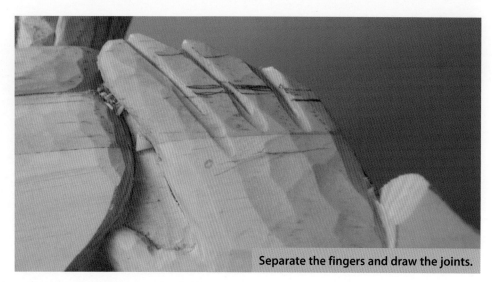

**Separate the fingers and draw the joints.**

gouge between each knuckle to make a depression. Scoop out a slight depression below the knuckles (toward the wrist) with a #5 12mm. With the #11 7mm, round the knuckles. Carve the other hand. Carve the saw marks off the side of the fingers, crown, and heart.

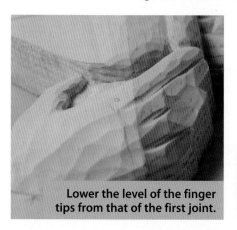

**Lower the level of the finger tips from that of the first joint.**

**Round the fingers.**

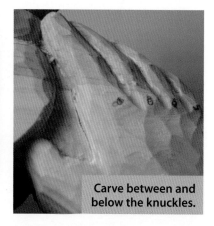

**Carve between and below the knuckles.**

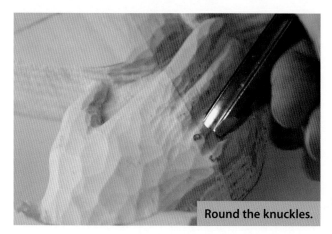

**Round the knuckles.**

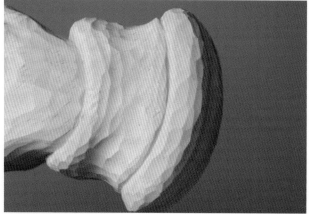

## 6 Carve the cuff.
Round the cuff using a #7 14mm chisel, taking care to scoop out the middle of the cuff. Round over the bottom of the cuff and carve the edge of the cuff to clean off the saw marks. Draw the cuff trim line ⅝" (16mm) from the edge, stop-cut with a V-groove, and round both edges into the stop cut. Carve the other cuff.

## CARVE THE HEART

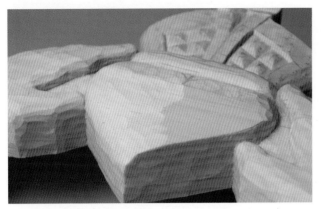

1 **Round and texture the surface.** Begin rounding the left edge of the heart using a #3 14mm fishtail. Round other side of the heart and texture the surface with a chisel so it matches the rest of the carving—if you don't do this, the difference will really show up when finishing the piece. Draw in the top of the heart and the centerline.

2 **Carve the top of the heart.** Round the top part into the centerline. Stop-cut the centerline at the top of the heart with a V-groove. Using a #3 14mm, round-over the top part of the heart into the stop cut. After rounding the other side, use the #11 7mm to clean and blend the point of the curve.

## ATTACH THE SIGN PIECES

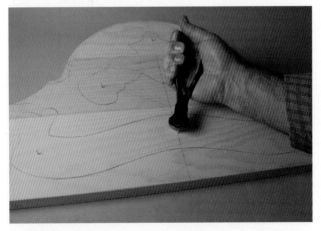

1 **Drive nails.** Drive #16 finish nails ½" (13mm) into the areas shown and clip the heads off to make a pointed end. These will hold the pieces in place while the glue dries.

2 **Glue the pieces.** After applying good quality exterior glue (such as System 3 T-88) to the backs of the banner and the claddagh, place them on the nails, lining them up as closely as possible to the outlines you drew before. Push the carvings down with an even pressure onto the background piece. Clamp the banner and claddagh to the background piece. After the glue has dried, clean the excess glue from the sign with an old chisel. This will save work sanding later.

## BASECOAT THE SIGN

**1 Apply the basecoat.**
Apply 3 coats of exterior latex primer. When dry, apply 3 more coats of exterior black latex paint. Basecoat the claddagh with 2–3 coats of a light yellow exterior latex paint. Basecoat the banner with 3 coats of Putnam ivory exterior latex. The yellow will act as a base for the gold leaf. The black background will be a good base for the smalt (crushed black glass). It is a rich finish that will accent the gold leafing.

## SHADE THE BANNER

Taking the extra time and effort to add shading to the banner will add much detail and dimension to your sign. You will be glad you took this extra step. It will take your project from an amateur effort to a professional product.

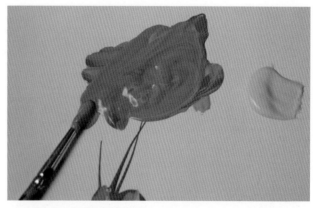

**1 Mix the shade.** Mix 1 part Putnam ivory to 1 part tan to make the paint for the banner.

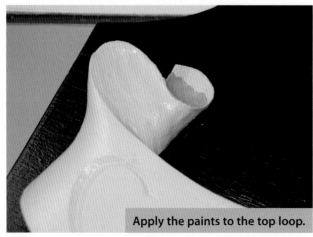

Apply the paints to the top loop.

**2 Paint the top two loops of the curl.** Paint Putnam ivory on the outside portion of the curl. Paint the mix on the inside curve. Blend the two colors well, so there is no line or separation between the two colors. Repeat this technique to shade the large curl below the top loop. Paint the loops on the right end of the banner in the same way.

Blend the top loop and apply the paints to the large curl.

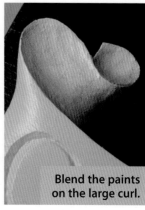

Blend the paints on the large curl.

3 **Shade other areas of the banner.** Paint the shade color in the center of the banner curve as shown, with the Putnam ivory around it. Blend. Do the same on the opposite end of the banner. Paint the shade color in the center of the banner, with the Putnam ivory painted to the left. Blend well. Add a bit more shade color to center of banner if it seems too dry, and paint the Putnam ivory to the right of it. Blend well.

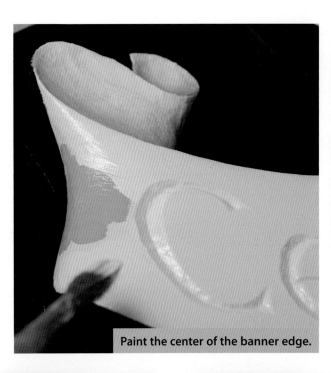

Paint the center of the banner edge.

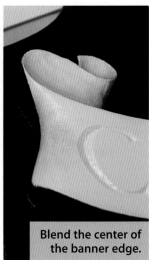

Blend the center of the banner edge.

Paint the center of the banner.

Blend the center of the banner.

4 **Clean up the edges.** Use the black latex paint to clean up the edge of the banner. Notice how the banner is made to look thin by painting the edge of it to match the background.

## PAINT THE SHAMROCK AND LETTERS

The letters and shamrock will be painted using the Sign Painter's One Shot Lettering Enamel used in previous projects. The shamrock will be shaded slightly.

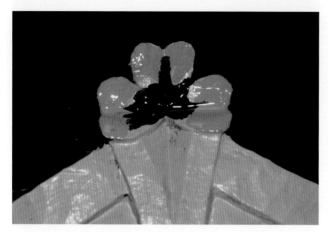

**1 Paint the shamrock.** The green on the shamrock is a mix of 1 part black, 1 part dark green, and 2 parts yellow. Use sign painter's enamel lettering paint. Paint the edges of the shamrock yellow and the center the dark green mix. Blend.

**2 Paint the letters.** Paint the letters with the dark green lettering enamel mix.

## GILD THE CLADDAGH

We will be using 23-karat gold leaf on the claddagh. This can be obtained from most art supply stores, as well as sign supply companies. Either of these can also supply the size, which is the glue that holds the gold leaf onto the surface it's applied to. It is commonly assumed that gold is a paint. There are gold paints available, but it has been my experience that they turn a dark unreadable brown after a short exposure to the weather. Those are best for indoor use. Gold leaf is actually hammered metal. It has a small amount of copper mixed in for strength. You can also buy 10-, 12-, or 18-karat gold leaf, but the luster is not as good. Gold is a surprisingly long-lasting material—it will only be affected by water or rot from the inside of the sign, and it doesn't wear or weather away.

This is a package of gold leaf, opened to show the 3⅜" x 3⅜" (86mm x 86mm) squares of patent leaf. "Patent leaf" means that the gold is slightly adhered to paper, which comes off easily when the leaf is applied to the size. I recommend starting with this as opposed to loose leaf, which is hard to handle.

I have found that mixing the size with the One Shot chrome yellow sign painter's paint in a 3 parts size to 2 parts yellow enamel paint ratio is the best way to apply size. I use size with a three-hour drying time. There are many other drying times available, but this works best for me. Since weather conditions can cause the time to vary greatly, I can apply it in the morning and know that it will set up sometime during the day. The gold needs to be applied to the size when it is almost, but not quite, dry. This is the only tricky part to gold leafing. If the size is too wet, the gold will dissolve slightly into the size and lose its luster. If the size is too dry, the gold leaf won't stick at all.

**1** **Apply the size.** Paint the size mixture onto the claddagh, taking care to apply a thin, even coat. I used a #6 round synthetic brush for this. As you paint, go over previously painted areas to clean out crevasses where the paint collects. The gold will stick wherever the size is. The size can be ready in 1-2 hours on a hot summer day, or 4-6 hours on a cold rainy day, so keep testing it. Do this with a knuckle on the back of your finger—don't ever use your fingertip, because the oils will affect the gold. Size that is ready should whistle when you pull your knuckle across it—it's the feeling you would get from a varnished tabletop that is almost dry, but still curing. If you put a glass on it, you know it might stick.

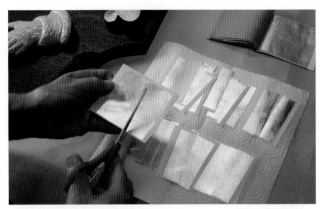

**2** **Prepare the gold.** Prepare the gold for use by cutting it in smaller widths with a clean pair of scissors. You will waste less gold when fitting it in tight places. I always use the patent gold, not the loose leaf. Patent gold comes adhered to a thin piece of paper that readily releases the gold to the size when lightly rubbed on to the sized surface.

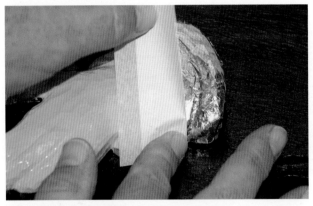

**3** **Apply the gold leaf.** Begin by laying the sheet of gold face down on the carving and lightly rubbing it on with your finger. When you feel you have rubbed the whole surface of the sheet, lift off the paper. Continue gilding, covering the claddagh carving.

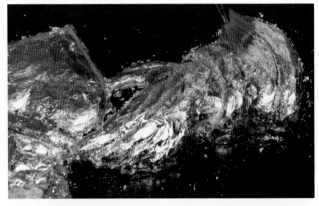

**4** **Tamp the gold.** After the whole surface is covered in gold, take a new soft brush and gently tamp the gold so all the crevasses are covered in gold. Gently sweep the excess gold off the black background. I save mine in a jar for touch-ups and gilding small Christmas ornaments. Wipe off the remaining gold dust. I like to use a baby wipe for this. Don't use baby wipes on the gold leafed claddagh!

**5** **Paint a black edge around the gold.** Use the black latex to paint a clean edge around the gold.

**6** **Paint the edge of the sign.** Using a mix of 1 part dark green lettering enamel to 3 parts yellow and 1 part black, paint the beveled edge of the sign. Let dry.

# ADD THE SMALT

Smalt is a crushed glass material and one use is to be applied as a finish to a sign, producing a beautiful and very durable top coating. It was a very widely used finish in the early 1870's and makes for a unique effect on a sign.

1 **Prepare the smalt.** Make a sifter from a plastic container by drilling or cutting some ⅛" (3mm) holes in the bottom. Test to make sure the smalt will come out in a steady steam.

2 **Apply paint.** When the sign edge is dry, paint the black background with a thick coat of black sign painter's enamel right up to the base of the claddagh. Do not paint the black edge of the claddagh.

Apply smalt.

3 **Apply smalt.** When the entire background surface is coated with paint, pour the smalt into the sifter and begin sifting the smalt onto the sign. Be sure to cover the entire surface in a thick coat. Let sit at least 24 hours to completely dry.

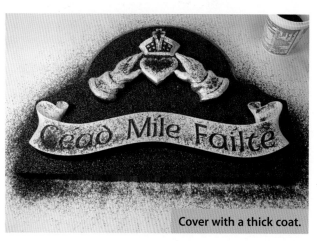

Cover with a thick coat.

4 **Clean off excess smalt.** When completely dry (in a day or so), slowly tip the sign up and let the smalt that did not stick fall off. Be sure to have a large piece of paper under the sign, so any smalt can be easily returned to the container when done. Gently brush off any remaining unattached smalt.

# CHAPTER 6:
# THE NEXT LEVEL

The following five projects are presented in a condensed form. If you've followed along through the first five chapters, you should now have a good understanding of the basic sign-carving and painting techniques I use. Apply what you've learned to these next five sign projects. By the time you're done, you'll pick up a few more tricks and tips for different styles of signs.

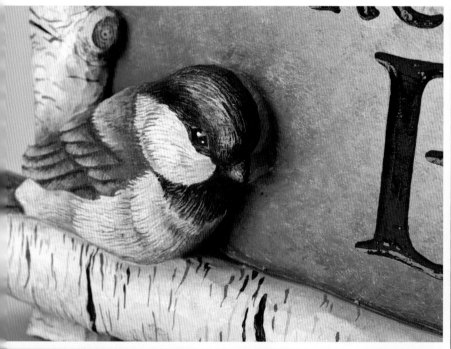

# BANNER *with a* RAISED STEIN

This malt beverage-inspired sign is designed to accent the home bar or rec room. I think it's a fun project, and would make a great gift as well. You'll get practice carving a larger banner, as well as what I call a free-form sign—one with no background. The multi-layered blank, which is used here to form the stein, is another great tool to use for dimensional signs.

## MATERIALS & TOOLS

- (1) Pine blank, 28" x 11½" x 1¾" (711mm x 292mm x 45mm), for the banner
- (1) Pine blank, 8½" x 9½" x 1¾" (216mm x 241mm x 45mm), for the stein
- #9 25mm chisel
- #5 30mm chisel
- #11 7mm chisel
- #11 10mm chisel
- V-groove chisel
- #3 14mm fishtail
- #8 25mm chisel
- Standard selection of paintbrushes: rounds, flats, script liners

- 1" and 1½" (25mm and 38mm) bristle brushes, for blending large areas
- Paints, California latex: gumleaf (light sage), Hawthorne Valley (dark sage), Essex green (very dark green), white, superior bronze (dark tan-gray), universal khaki (light tan-gray), tattersol brown, black
- One Shot sign painter's enamel: Ivory
- Glue: exterior or interior, as appropriate

**Stein pattern**
Photocopy at 150%

Please note that patterns are given only for the ends of the scroll—please adjust the length of the scroll based on the text you'd like to appear on it.

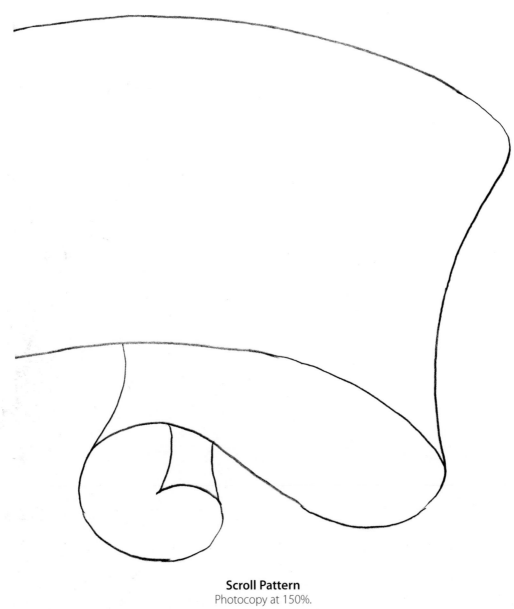

**Scroll Pattern**
Photocopy at 150%.

**1 Customize the pattern.** To begin this project, it's best to scan it right into the computer to both enlarge it to the proper size and lay out the lettering at the same time, using whatever program you like. I prefer CorelDraw 12; it is very good at manipulating text. Of course, you can also do it by hand. Because the curve of this banner is more complex, you will need to spend more time in adjusting the letters. Choose a straight font, not an italic one—they don't work well on a curve. If working with a computer program, remember to outline the letters and remove the fill to cut down on the ink you use printing.

**2 Transfer the pattern to the blank.** After you've drawn or printed out the complete pattern with the lettering, trace out the banner and stein—don't bother tracing the letters yet. For the stein, make sure the grain is running vertically. The banner's grain should be horizontal.

**3 Cut out the blanks.** Cut out the two pieces. Note there is no handle on the stein. We will carve the handle out of extra material from the banner. Place the stein on the banner and trace its outline; this will make for a better match. Don't glue the pieces together; we will carve them separately and glue later on.

**Cut a deep trench through the banner. Note the pencil depth lines.**

**4 Carve the banner.** Draw a curve on the side of the banner: near the stein, it is about 1" (25mm) from the top, and curves gradually up to the surface right before the right-end curls. The right-end curl will drop ½" (13mm). The loop to the left of the right-end curl should have a mark ¾" (19mm) down from the surface. Use a #9 25mm chisel to cut a deep trench through the banner next to the handle (see above). Use a #5 30mm chisel to carve down the surface of the banner to the lines. Cut away the excess material next to the handle. Carve away the material inside the handle, beginning with a #11 10mm to scoop out as much as possible, and finish with a V-groove and #3 14mm fishtail. Draw a level line for the bevel of the left-end curl down 1" (25mm) from the surface and bevel the curl from the banner edge (see right). Redraw the curls on the banner and carve them. Round-over the top roll of the banner, and scoop out the low parts. See the claddagh project if you need a reminder. When you've completed the carving of the banner, sand it and trace on the letters.

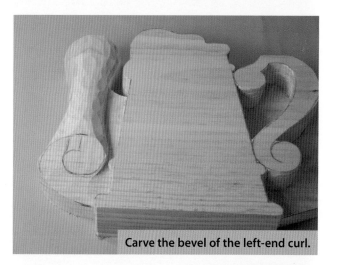

**Carve the bevel of the left-end curl.**

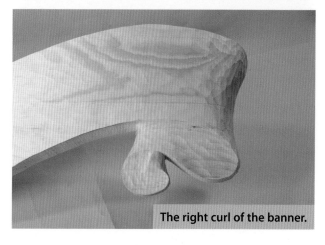

**The right curl of the banner.**

**Carve the slope of the stein's surface and cut around the foam.**

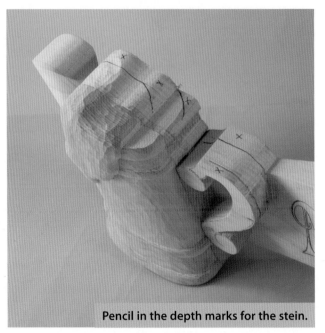

**Pencil in the depth marks for the stein.**

**5** **Carve the stein.** Draw a straight diagonal line on the side of the stein that begins at the top line of the bottom lip and slopes down to 1" (25mm) below the top of the upper lip. V-cut around the bottom of the foam and bevel the surface of the mug down to the depth line. Round-over the stein and round the bottom lip. Draw on the raised rib lines; use a V-groove to stop-cut and lower the area between the ribs ¼" (6mm). Round the top of the foam slightly and glue the stein onto the banner. When the glue has dried, complete the shaping of the foam. Draw lines on the side of the handle ¼" (6mm) down from top and up from the back to the same level as the banner (see above right).

On the foam, draw a line ½" (13mm) up from the back and remove this extra material. Carve the handle and make sure you are happy with the shape of the foam. Carve the letters, using stop cut lines and grain direction lines as a guide.

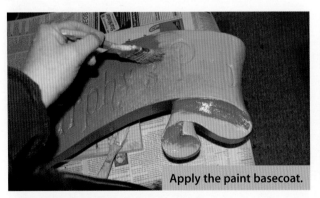

**Apply the paint basecoat.**

**Paint the left-end curls.**

**6** **Prime and basecoat the sign.** Once the sign has been painted with three coats of primer, apply the basecoat. I am choosing light and dark tones of a sage green for the banner, a warm gray for the stein, and a warm white for the foam. Place the sign so it is accessible from all sides—I'm using a Workmate bench—and raise it up off the surface using the scrap lumber with nails driven in. Paint the portion of the banner closest to the stein (the low part) with the Hawthorne Valley dark sage, and the rest of the banner (the high part) with Gumleaf light sage. Blend using the bristle brushes. Now paint the dark sage at the top of each curl and the light sage at the lower edge of each curl and blend. Paint the left-end curls with dark and light sage in the areas shown in the photo above and blend. Paint the stein with the Universal Khaki light warm gray. Paint the foam white. Let dry.

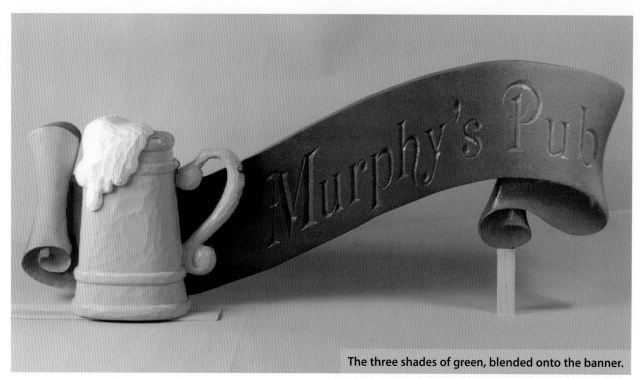

**The three shades of green, blended onto the banner.**

7 **Apply the final coat of paint to the banner.** Paint the darkest green (Essex Green) on the third of the banner nearest the stein. Paint the dark sage (Hawthorne Valley) on the center third and the light sage (Gumleaf) on the right third. Blend these well with a large bristle brush. Paint and blend the curls. Paint the low area right next to the stein Essex Green. Paint the curled banner top with light and dark sage where shown (right) and blend. Shade the middle of the left end of the banner.

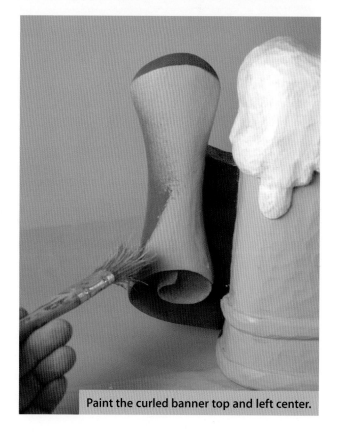

**Paint the curled banner top and left center.**

**8** **Apply the final coat of paint to the stein.** Paint superior bronze dark tan-gray on the sides of the stein, coming up higher on the left side (see right). Paint universal khaki light tan-gray in the center. Blend. Add white a little to the right of center down the length of the stein and blend.

**Paint the stein with dark tan-gray on the sides and the lighter tan-gray in the middle.**

**Paint the handle.**

Apply the light and dark tones to the handle—dark on the sides and light in the center—and blend. Add a little white to the handle and round elements, and blend in slightly.

**Apply the shadow tone to the foam.**

Mix 1 part white to 1 part Tattersol brown. This is the shadow color for the foam that goes under the round drips, in any depressions, and on the sides. Paint this color on the foam as seen above. Paint the rest of the foam white and blend the two. Let the stein dry. Mix 1 part black to 1 part superior bronze. Paint this on the stein under the foam and blend with a damp blending brush. Do the same on the left edge of the stein and under the round bands.

**9** **Paint the letters.** Paint the letters with the One Shot sign painter's enamel in ivory.

# OVAL SIGN *with* DUCK

This sign design would be suitable for a wide variety of home styles, and could be customized with many different kinds of wildlife or objects: for example, a raised pineapple looks great in the oval on top. To make this sign, you'll practice using a string and pins to lay out an oval, carving a raised object, and texturing with a Dremel tool.

## MATERIALS & TOOLS

- (1) Pine blank, 16" x 18½" x 1¼" (406mm x 470mm x 32mm), for sign
- (1) Pine blank, 5½" x 10" x 1¾" (140mm x 254mm x 45mm), for duck
- Scrap pieces of ¾" (19mm) pine, for cattails
- Cotton twine, 24" (610mm) long
- Ruler
- #18 brads
- (3) Thumbtacks
- Pencil
- #11 10mm chisel
- #11 5mm chisel
- V-groove
- Skew
- #15 6mm V-groove
- #3 3mm chisel
- #3 5mm chisel

- #15 6mm chisel
- #3 8mm fishtail
- Dremel tool
- ¼" (6mm) rough ruby bit
- ¼" (6mm) diamond bit
- ⅛" (3mm) cylindrical diamond bit
- #15 6mm V-groove
- #3 8mm chisel
- #5 8mm chisel
- #8 7mm chisel
- Sign painter's enamel paints: bright red, chrome yellow, dark green
- Paints, California latex: white, tan, Newport blue, wooden oar, muddy river, black, evening velvet, yellow, Essex green
- Exterior epoxy or glue

Add

Left wing

Drop ⅞"

Add

1

Add

2

Add

1

1

1

2

1

3

1

**Duck pattern**
Photocopy at 150%.

Start carving leaves
numbered *1* and proceed
on to *2* and *3*. Leaf stop
cuts in red. Stems and
tips of cattails are all *1*.

**Duck Point Text**
Photocopy at 125%.

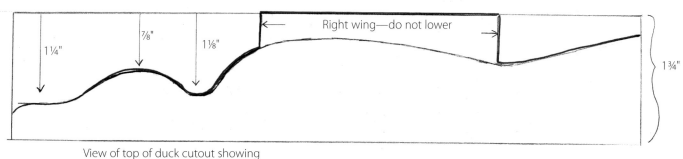

1¼"    ⅞"    1⅛"    Right wing—do not lower    1¾"

View of top of duck cutout showing
initial levels to drop carving to.

**1** **Lay out the duck and letters.** Trace the duck pattern on its blank. The thinner parts of the duck (bill and tail) should be oriented so the grain direction is the strongest, a.k.a. parallel to the tail and bill. Although enlarging the sign pattern will give you an oval, you will get a perfect, more even oval by drawing one using a string and pins. Draw the centerline top to bottom. Measure up from the bottom 1¼" (32mm) and draw a letter line. The letter space is 2¾" (70mm) high and 14½" (368mm) long. The font used here is BD Santa Monica. Trace on the letters.

**2** **Draw the oval with a string and pins.** See sidebar.

**3** **Finish laying out the sign.** Draw a slightly smaller oval inside this one by marking ½" (13mm) from the big oval line all the way around and connecting the marks. A see-through quilter's ruler is ideal for this. This will be the beveled edge. To draw the curved shoulder of the sign, measure in 3¾" (95mm) from the edge and up 8¼" (210mm) from the bottom. This should be on the oval. Place a protractor, round dessert plate, or gallon paint can so it hits both points and draw the curve. Repeat on other side. Cut out the blanks on the band saw.

**Draw the oval.**

# HOW TO DRAW AN OVAL

**1** Determine size of oval—here, 13 ½" x 10" (343mm x 254mm).

**2** Measure and draw horizontal and vertical center lines, shown here in red.

**3** Place a tack ⅛" (3mm) in from the left or right side of the horizontal line, shown here in green.

**4** From this point, measure diagonally to the vertical line where half the vertical measurement, here 6¾" (172mm), intersects it (shown in green).

**5** Place another tack here, shown as a purple dot. Repeat steps 4 and 5 to plot the placement for the tack below the center line.

**6** Tie a string as tightly as you can around the perimeter formed by the three tacks.

**7** Remove the tack on the horizontal line (the one represented by the green dot) and place the pencil tip into the string loop at that point.

**8** Pull the pencil outward toward the edge of the sign and maintain this firm, outward pull while also drawing the oval.

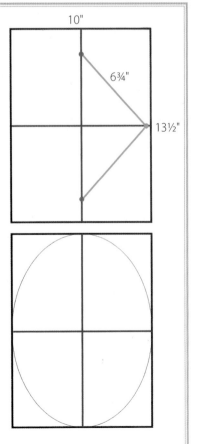

CHAPTER 6: THE NEXT LEVEL

**4** **Carve the duck.** Drop the back wing of the duck to ⅜" (10mm) from the bottom with a #11 10mm chisel. V-groove the line separating the two wings. Draw the duck's body shape on the top. Use the pattern on page 128 as a reference. You may need to move the pattern as you go. When done tracing, remove the excess material by cutting straight through. Begin rounding the body and the neck, using the V-groove to stop cut the edges of the wing from the body. Looking down at the top of the tail, draw the curved feather line and remove the excess. Use a #11 5mm to cut a horizontal groove through the eye area. Lower the top of the head above the groove. Round the cheek and top of the head, dropping the height of each ⅛" (3mm). Taper the head down toward the bill, leaving the cheek high at the back. Draw on the eye and bill. V-cut the line separating the bill and drop the bill ⅛" (3mm). Shape the bill. Shape the eye; it should curve gently from top to bottom, and deeper side to side, into the corners.

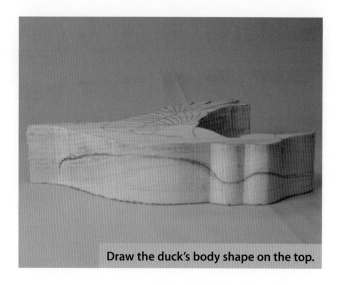

**Draw the duck's body shape on the top.**

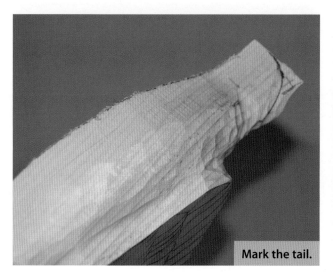

**Mark the tail.**

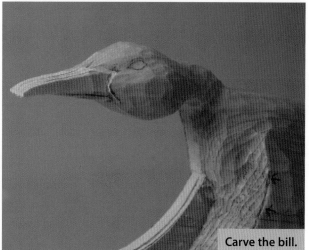

**Carve the bill.**

**5** **Carve the tail and wing.** Draw the feathers on the tail and trim ends. Use the #15 6mm V-groove to separate the feathers from the body and from one another. Bevel each feather down into the cut slightly.

Redraw the feathers on the wing and use a V-groove to stop cut the feather edges of the top row. Bevel the entire bottom row down to the stop cut. Repeat for the next row. Number the feathers as shown (right). Use your #15 6mm to stop cut each feather edge. Bevel each feather toward the next, beginning with #1. Use your skew to make a small stop cut at the top of each feather so the wood chip will come off cleanly. Tuck the feathers in using a #3 8mm fishtail. Each feather will bevel down ⅛" (3mm).

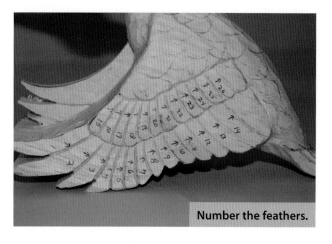

**Number the feathers.**

**6** **Texture the feathers.** Begin by drawing the feather shapes on the back of the duck and shape them into bumps with the Dremel and a ¼" (6mm) rough ruby bit. Repeat with a ¼" (6mm) diamond bit to smooth the entire surface of the bumps and the body. Use the Dremel to form the eyelids close to the eye on the duck as well.

Draw the feather texture on the wings and body of the duck as shown (center). Using a ⅛" (3mm) cylindrical diamond bit, (see instruction in Chapter 4), stone the texture for the feathers with a quick flicking motion.

**7** **Carve the cattails.** Cut out and round the three raised cattails. Put the finished duck carving and the raised cattails in place and trace around them. Draw the stop cuts on the leaves and letters.

**8** **Chip-carve the leaves and letters.** Stop-cut the veins in number order. Carve the leaves by beveling the lower edge into the stop cut using a #3 8mm and a #5 8mm. Note the directional carving arrows based on the grain direction. Once the lower side is done, begin on the upper side. Switch to a #8 7mm if a curve in the leaf fits it. When a leaf folds over, scoop out the two fold portions. Stop-cut the ends of the stems where they tuck under another item and scoop. Carve the cattails' points. Carve the sign's bevel. Carve the letters.

**9** **Attach the duck and cattails.**

**10** **Prep for painting.** After the glue dries, unclamp, clean the edges, and sand. Prime with three coats of latex paint.

**11** **Apply the basecoat to the sky.** Flip the sign over on its face and paint the back and sides with three coats of muddy river. Basecoat the sky portion of the sign with a mix of 1½ parts white to 1 part Newport blue. Be sure to paint the sky color up on the entire side surface of the wings all the way to the top, and paint ⅛" (3mm) up on the cattails and duck body. Paint the background of the lettered area with 3 coats of muddy river.

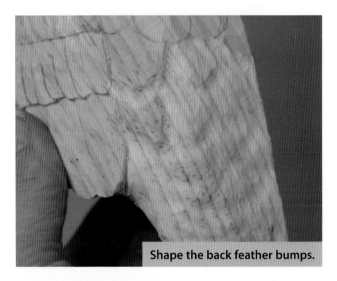
Shape the back feather bumps.

Draw the feather texture.

Chip-carve the leaves.

**12** Apply finish paint to the sky. Mix a darker tone of sky with 1½ parts Newport blue to 1 part white. Paint this in three spots, and paint the lighter mix used for the basecoat on the rest of the sky. Blend with a sweeping motion back and forth across the sky.

While the sky is still wet, use a round bristle blender to add some clouds. Tap one part of the brush into white. Hold brush so the white is on the top, and jab the brush repeatedly with some force onto the wet sky paint. This will cause the top of the cloud to stay white and the bottom to blend into the sky for a great quick cloud. Try to paint them so they are broader at the bottom.

**13** Paint the water. Using the same dark and light sky blue, paint the water from the horizon down. Start with the dark blue and blend in the light as you go down.

**14** Basecoat the foliage and cattails. Basecoat the green foliage using a dark Essex green. I like to use an old blender brush whose bristles are splayed and split apart to achieve the texture here. After the base coat, tap the brush in some light green (made by mixing Essex green and yellow) and then on the right side of the foliage clumps. Tap in some white at the base of the foliage.

**15** Apply finish paint to rest of sign. When dry, start to finish paint the scene, starting at the tail. The cattails are tan, the stems a light tan (mix white and tan), and the leaves are light green. The duck's bill is yellow mixed with a little white; the duck's head is light green. The tail is white, as is the band around the neck. The chest is tan; the wings are a blend of muddy river at the feather tips and a mix of 2 parts white to 1 part muddy river for the feather tops, blended. The duck's back is a blend of these two tones of muddy river as well. There is a band of black at the end of the body near the tail, and evening velvet on the last 5 feathers on the first row of wing feathers. Study the image of the finished project and apply the painting knowledge you've learned from the other projects to finish painting the sign.

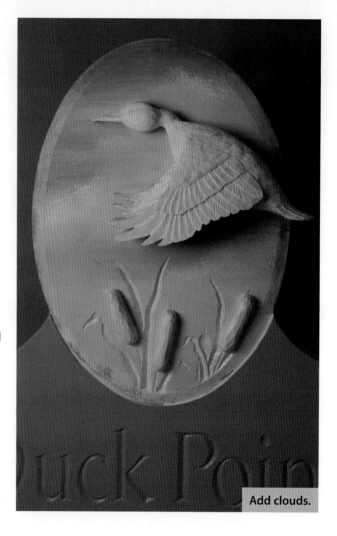

**Add clouds.**

# CABIN SIGN *with* BIRCH LOG FRAME

This unique sign is designed for a lodge-style cabin, but could be used for any woodsy or nature-loving home. The birch frame is both impressive and relatively easy to achieve. You'll experiment with using a router to lower areas, and carve and detail a small bird.

## MATERIALS & TOOLS

- (1) Pine blank, 11" x 23½" x 1¾" (279mm x 597mm x 45mm)
- Router
- ½" router bit
- Safety glasses
- Dust mask
- Clamps
- #15 6mm V-groove
- #3 14mm fishtail
- #9 10mm chisel
- Skew
- #11 5mm chisel
- #8 7mm chisel
- #3 3mm chisel
- #3 5mm chisel
- #11 10mm chisel
- Enamel paint colors: Dark blue and dark green.
- Latex colors: White, Newport blue, wooden oar, muddy river, tan yellow, red, black, Essex green.
- Selection of paintbrushes

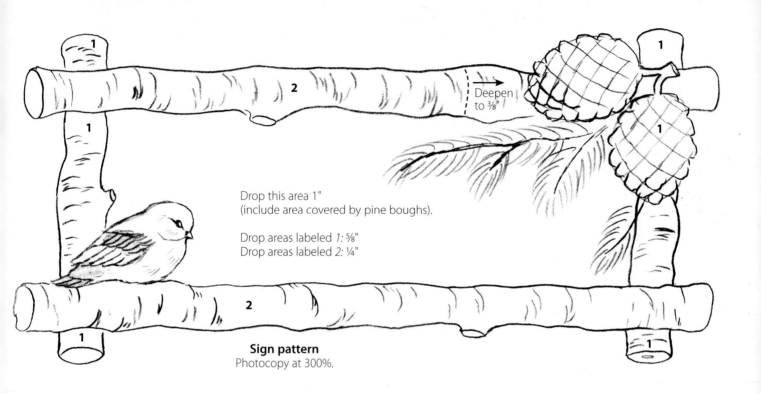

Deepen to ⅜"

Drop this area 1"
(include area covered by pine boughs).

Drop areas labeled *1*: ⅝"
Drop areas labeled *2*: ¼"

**Sign pattern**
Photocopy at 300%.

**Sign Text**
Photocopy at 200%.

CHAPTER 6: THE NEXT LEVEL

# Making the Cabin Sign with Birch Log Frame

1  **Prepare the sign blank.** Enlarge the pattern to the appropriate size. Trace on the bird, pinecones, and birch logs. Use a band saw to cut out the shape of the sign.

2  **Use a router to drop the sign background.** The background of the sign needs to drop 1" (25mm). Although some people prefer to use a chisel, it is faster and cleaner to use a router. I recommend a 1½ horsepower router. The level of the background should be taken down in stages to avoid burning the tip of the bit. The bit should be set no deeper than ½" (13mm) for the first pass. Secure the blank firmly to a stable bench and clamp it down, being sure that the clamps will not interfere with the plate on the router as it moves over the surface of the sign.

Hold the router handles with your forearms on the table for control. The little rectangle in the tool will be your view of what the router will be cutting. Start by going around the border; then start removing wood with steady passes.

When using a router on this large an area, you need to leave some raised platforms to support the router plate and prevent it from falling into the routered-out area. After completing the first pass at ½" (13mm), increase the depth on the bit to 1" (25mm) and go over the area again to deepen. Use a wide chisel to remove the platforms left by the router.

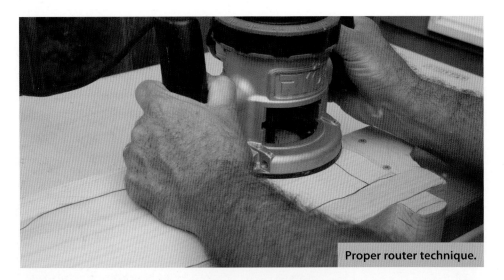

Proper router technique.

It is important to leave platforms of wood for the router to rest on.

**3** **Label and mark drops.** Label the sign parts as shown on the pattern (page 135). Draw the level lines on all the edges: Areas labeled "1" should drop ⅝" (16mm) from the surface. Areas labeled "2" will drop ¼" (6mm) from the surface. You can drop the area under or next to the pinecones to slightly deeper than ¼" to ⅜" (6mm to 10mm).

**4** **Carve the log frame.** Stop-cut the lines where the logs labeled "1" meet the pine cones, bird, and logs labeled "2"; use the #15 6mm V-groove. Drop the logs labeled "1" and "2" to the levels drawn using a #3 14mm fishtail. Stop-cut the lower log ends free and round from side to side, but leave the ends uncarved. Repeat for all the lower log ends. Gouge around the branch that protrudes from the log with a #9 10mm; round from side to side, leaving the end alone. Round over the log on the left. Draw on the beveled end on the bottom of the log, as well as the splits in the log. These will be cut with the #15 V-groove. Bevel the end of the log and branch to the level drawn.

After cutting the splits in the log, gouge slightly beside each cut so they look more open. Stop-cut the edge of the pinecone from the top log and round the log from side to side as shown. Don't round over the end. Draw and bevel the log ends. Draw on the splits in the top and bottom logs and cut.

**Carve the bevel on the log end.**

TIP

### Fixing a Fracture in the Curved Frame

When you encounter a curve in the shape of the log, the grain will cause some fracturing. This can be frustrating, because the "change direction if it fractures" rule won't work. When you have reached the point where the two fractures meet, use a #7 14mm or #8 25mm to carve it from a right angle to the other cuts, as shown here.

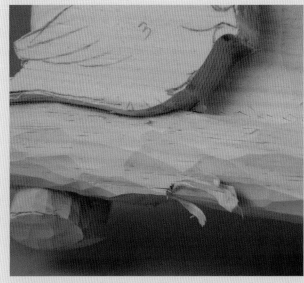

A fracture in the wood.

Come at it from a right angle to the original cuts.

5 **Carve the pinecones.** Begin rounding the pinecones. Stop-cut the tops to free up the stems, tucking them under the pinecone edge. Round each stem and cut in the bevel at the end. Draw the curved lines from the pinecone top to bottom. The scales overlap each other and the points alternate like lollipop shingles on a house roof. Draw on the scales, having the pointed ends begin where the top of the one below ended. Be sure the scales get larger as they reach the center, and begin to shrink as they go from the center to the top. Use the V-groove to stop-cut the scales. Number the scales, starting with the tip as "1" and making each successive row the next number. Beginning with "1," bevel the scales down to the edge of the one above. Use a skew to stop cut the corners and to take out the chips left there. Continue to carve the scales in order, moving up the pinecone as you go.

**Finished pinecone on the right.**

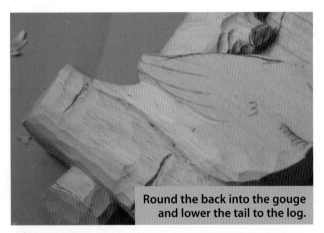

**Round the back into the gouge and lower the tail to the log.**

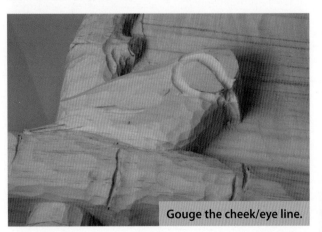

**Gouge the cheek/eye line.**

6 **Carve the bird.** Round the belly over in the direction of the arrows. Clean the shape under the chin with a #11 5mm. Tuck the body under the wing. Stop-cut and round the body and tail.

Draw the gouge line between the tail and back; carve in the gouge with a #8 7mm. Round the bird's back into the gouge and lower the tail so it rests on the log. Gouge the line drawn under the cheek and round the belly up to the gouge. Round the back and wing. Draw tail feathers on. Use the #8 7mm to gouge a separation between the beak and the head of the bird. Drop the beak ⅛" (3mm). Round the bill over and point the end.

Draw the line shown around the cheek and through the eye. Gouge this line with a #11 5mm and drop the top of the head to the gouge level. Round over the top of the head. Draw on feather detail. Gouge lines drawn on the chest, back, and near the tail with the #8 7mm (see below).

Round edges made with the gouge. Draw the edges of the wing feathers and trim them. Stop-cut under the upper row of feathers with the V-groove and tuck the first row down to the stop cut. Draw the feathers back in. V-cut the feathers and number them as shown. Bevel the feathers into the stop cut. Draw on the eye. Stop-cut with the skew and round over. The #3 3mm and 5mm are great for this. Draw on the feather detail for stoning. Stone the feather texture with cylindrical bits.

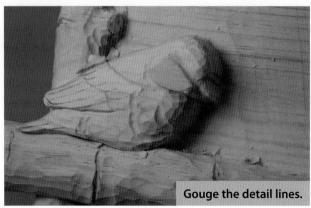

**Gouge the detail lines.**

**7** **Undercut the elements.** The look of the sign can be greatly improved by rounding over the pinecones and logs, and undercutting them and the bird. Undercutting is simply continuing to round over the object a little more. Draw a curved line on the edge of the pinecone, and also, turn the sign over to draw the log behind the pinecone. We will drop the pinecone with a #9 10 mm gouge to these two lines (see right).

Deepen the gouge with a #11 10mm and round the pinecone from the back. Draw the scales around the side and carve as before. Repeat this for the other pinecone. Round the back of the logs, starting with the ends. Turn the sign over and draw the short side logs over the protruding ends of the long top and bottom logs. V-cut the edges of the end of the logs and round them over. Continue rounding the rest of the logs from the back. Undercut the inside edges of the logs with the V-groove.

**The undercut pinecone creates a lot of dimension.**

**8** **Carve the letters.** Trace on the letters you have chosen for the sign. Before printing out the name you want, be sure to measure the area so they fit. I have chosen a font with rounded ends, called Worcester Rout, because I want to scoop the letters instead of V-cutting them. Scooping the letters is a fast way of carving them. You use mainly one or two chisels, usually #11 5mm or larger. Carve by gouging up the letter, concentrating on one side of the letter at a time. Start serifs from the outer edge and scoop into the center, blending the scoop in. The key here is to carefully cut the edges of each letter as straight as possible. This will be essential to painting a clean straight line later.

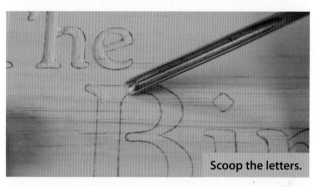

**Scoop the letters.**

**9** **Prime the sign with three coats of latex primer.**

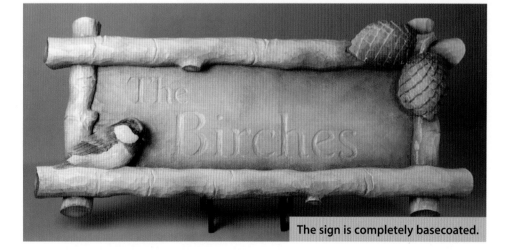

**The sign is completely basecoated.**

**10** **Apply basecoat to the sign.** Basecoat the sky by first mixing 1 part Newport blue to 4 parts white; paint this in the center of the sign and Newport Blue around the edges. Blend with a 1½" (38mm) bristle brush. Basecoat the logs by blending white in the middle of the log, muddy river around the white, and wooden oar under the logs, bird, and on the edges. Blend with a large bristle brush. Continue blending the logs with these three colors. Basecoat the pinecones: paint the center white; paint a ring around the center using a mix of 1 part tan to 1 part white; paint a final ring of tan. Blend. Paint the cut ends of the logs with white in the center and tan around the edge and blend. Basecoat the bird's chest: Paint the upper chest white; mix tan with a little yellow and white, paint that on the lower body, and blend. Paint the wing a brown made by mixing 1½ parts yellow to 1 part red and 1 part black. Highlight with white and blend. Paint the cap on the chickadee black and highlight with white at the top. Blend. Take care to paint the shape of the cap dipping under the eye, curving back up around the cheek, and then to a point in the back.

11 **Finish painting the sky.** Repeat the same painting steps as in the basecoat, except add more Newport blue to the edge and to the areas behind the bird and around the pinecones. Blend.

12 **Paint the pinecones.** Using tan, paint the tops of each scale on the pinecone and blend with a damp brush. As you proceed to the darker edges of the pinecone, switch to a darker brown paint. When these dry, we will return to add a darker shade.

13 **Finish painting the logs.** Repaint the logs in the same way as the basecoat for a good solid cover. Mix 2 parts wooden oar to 3 parts black plus a little of the dark brown mix for a darker tone for the logs. Add this to the rounded undersides of the logs, and blend with a damp brush. Paint all the logs in this way. Let dry. Paint the ends of all the logs and branches in the same way as the base coat, with tan edges and white centers, blending as before. Load a script liner with a mix of tan and the dark brown mix, (and a little water if needed) and paint on the growth rings. Mix 1 part white to 1 part muddy river and load the script liner (add a little water if needed so the paint will flow better) and paint the shot bark lines on the logs as shown. Be sure to curve them in the same direction as the end of the log. Add some darker lines in the same way using wooden oar and also a few lines using the darkest mix (2 parts wooden oar to 3 parts black and a little dark brown) used to shade the logs. The lines should be a little wiggly. Mix 1 part black to 1 part dark brown and paint the V-grooves cut into the logs.

**Paint the top edges of the scales.**

**14** **Finish painting the sky.** Repeat the same painting steps as in the basecoat, except add more Newport blue to the edge and to the areas behind the bird and around the pinecones. Blend.

The added pine branches and the detail on the pinecones really pop.

**15** **Paint the bird.** Repaint the wings and tail in the same way as the basecoat: use a mix of 1½ parts yellow to 1 part red and 1 part black. Highlight each layer of feathers with white and blend. Paint the black bib under the chin. Mix 1 part black to 1 part of the brown and paint each upper half of the feather layers and blend with a damp brush. Add a little shading to the chest and cheek with the mix of 1 part yellow, 1 part tan, and a touch of red. Blend with a damp brush. Using a script liner, pull some of the body shading mix of tan and yellow up into the white areas above the shadow. Wash a mix of "dirty water" using a little wing brown with a lot of water, over the entire bird and let dry. Paint black on the cap and bib and highlight with white. Blend well. When dry, dry brush some white across the top and bib to highlight the stoning texture. Be sure to brush at right angles to the texture. Using a little dot of white on the tip of the script liner, add the glints to the eye. The last thing to do on the bird is to pull some of the white feathery edges into the wing or tail below them, and the black edges into the chest or cheek below those areas.

**16** **Paint the pine needles.** Begin painting the pine needles on the branches using Essex green thinned with a little water. I used a #4 script liner for this. Continue to paint a lighter layer of needles over these dark ones by using a mix of 1 part Essex green to 1 part yellow. Add a second layer by mixing 2 parts white to 1 part of this mixture. Add one more layer of light green if necessary.

**17** **Paint the letters.** Paint the letters with 1 part dark green to 1 part dark blue One Shot sign painter's paint.

# BEACH HOUSE SIGN

This colorful sign is designed for a beach vacation home. It's a lovely way to put a name to a special piece of property. You'll create a relief-carved landscape, and paint an advanced scene with a sunset sky.

## MATERIALS & TOOLS

- **(1) Pine blank, 19½" x 8½" x 1¾" (495mm x 216mm x 45mm)**
- **(1) Pine blank, 36" x 5½" x 1¾" (914mm x 140mm x 45mm)**
- **Router**
- **#15 6mm V-groove**
- **#9 10mm gouge**
- **#2 8mm**
- **One Shot sign painter's enamel: ivory**
- **Exterior latex paints: Newport blue, yellow, white, crimson red, tattersol brown, wooden oar, tomahawk**

**Lighthouse scene**
Photocopy at 200%.

**Sign text**

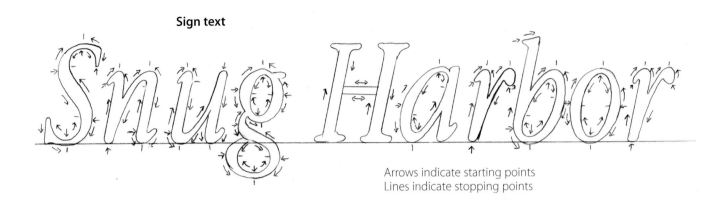

Arrows indicate starting points
Lines indicate stopping points

**Sign layout**

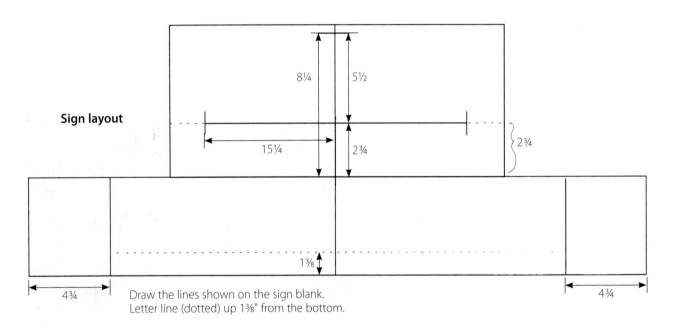

8¼  5½
15¼  2¾
2¾
1⅜
4¾  4¾

Draw the lines shown on the sign blank.
Letter line (dotted) up 1⅜" from the bottom.

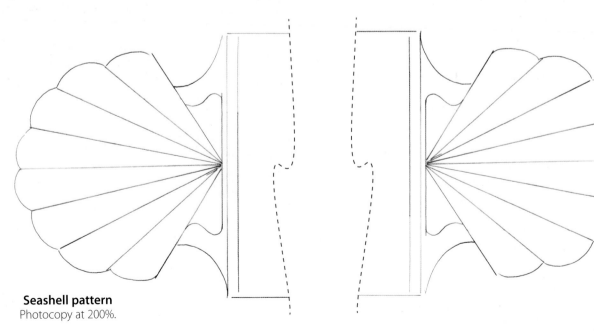

**Seashell pattern**
Photocopy at 200%.

**1** **Create the sign blank.** The sign blank needed for this project will be made with a longer piece of wood glued onto a shorter blank. I would glue up the smaller blank, 19½" x 8½" x 1¾" (495mm x 216mm x 45mm) first. When the first blank is dry, glue the 36" x 5½" x 1¾" (914mm x 140mm x 45mm) piece so it is centered on the first blank. Draw the lines shown on the illustration on page 144. Use the string and pins method described on page 130 to create the oval for the lighthouse scene. Measure 5¼" (133mm) from the center on the horizontal line. Measure 7⅝" (194mm) from that point to the vertical line. Proceed to create the oval as described earlier. Use the router to lower the sky portion of the scene down ¾" (19mm) from the surface. Cut the sign shape out on a band saw.

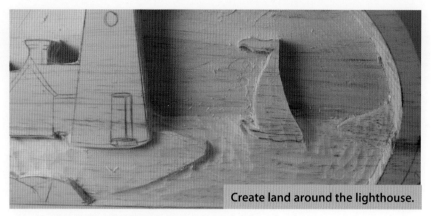

Create land around the lighthouse.

**2** **Rough-in the landscape.** Begin cleaning all the areas that the router couldn't get with a #15 6mm V-groove in the corners and a small #3 elsewhere. V-cut around the rocks, buildings, and bottom of the scene. Drop the water, boat, and land ¼" (6mm) from the surface.

Draw land around the lighthouse and gouge this line. Bevel the water down ⅛" (3mm) from the sky and draw in the boat hull and land on the right. Gouge around them and bevel the water to meet the horizon.

**3** **Carve the sailboat.** Begin by V-cutting the bottom of the sail free from the boat. Round over the belly of the sail to the left and down into the boat. V-cut the top of the bow of the boat and drop the water so the bow is free. V-cut the hull where it meets the water and round it under the wave. Gouge the place indicated on the flag and blend the edges. Lastly, round the top of the wave and blend the wave into the rest of the water with a #9 10mm gouge and cut the angle on the stern of the boat.

Carve the house.

Carve the lighthouse.

**4** **Carve the house.** Round-over the land, V-cutting the lighthouse and house to separate the land from them. Stop-cut and drop the two house sections to either side ⅜" (10mm) and round the lawn down to meet them. Stop-cut and drop both chimneys ½" (13mm). Bevel the two roof sections to meet the chimneys. Stop-cut the roofs to separate them from the front of the house. Draw on the chimney details and the window on the left part of the house. Drop the area behind the window 1/16" (3mm) and flatten the trim on the roof. Bevel the chimneys so the middle point is the highest. Drop the front portion of the chimney and bevel the edges above down to it. Drop the front of the house down to the lawn, slightly above the other house sections, and drop the trim down to be ⅙" (4mm) above the house. Bevel the edges on the trim toward the house. Draw in the door and window and drop 1/16" (3mm).

**5** **Carve the lighthouse.** Gouge over the area under the platform near the top of the lighthouse with a #9 10mm and bevel the surface of the lighthouse down to it. Round the sides of the lighthouse. Stop-cut the top of the lighthouse from the railing and drop the area ⅜" (10mm). Redraw the light top, drop it ⅛" (3mm), and round over the sides and top. Round both railings' sides and then correct the edges with a gouge. Draw in the window and door. Drop the shaded portion of the door ⅛" (3mm) and the window 1/16" (2mm). Bevel the door side into the door.

**6** **Carve the rocks.** Stop-cut and drop the rock on the left ⅛" (3mm) and redraw the line. Stop-cut the rock on the right and pitch the edge near the center rock down in the direction of the arrow. Pitch the two sides of the rock on the left to form a peak and cut in a few more angles using a #2 8mm chisel. Pitch the center rock in the directions of the arrows. Stop-cut using a skew around the edges of the frame, buildings, and boat where they are in front of the sky, and clean the router marks off by carving the entire sky surface with a #3 14mm fishtail. Stop-cut the lines of the fans drawn beside the frame with the V-groove and bevel them down in the direction of the arrows.

**The scene carving is complete.**

**7** **Carve the shell ends.** Begin by V-cutting the shell body from the hinges and bevel to the stop cut on the shell about ⅜" (10mm) deep. Redraw the hinges. Repeat on other shell. Stop-cut around the hinges and drop the surface behind them ⅛" (3mm). Round over the sides of the shell about ⅜"–½" (10–13mm) on the sides. Draw in rays extending from the point on the shell to the edge. V-cut the lines and round over as shown. Repeat on other shell.

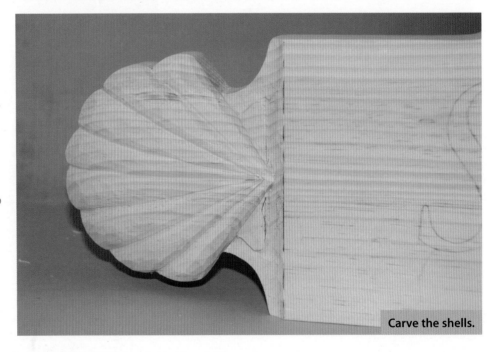

**Carve the shells.**

**8** **Carve the letters.** I have chosen a font that has rounded serifs, because I want to scoop the letters. Use a #11 7mm to scoop first one side and then the other in the direction of the arrows. Finish by scooping the center of the letter to clean.

**9** **Prime the entire sign with three coats of exterior latex primer.**

**Nearly complete basecoat.**

**10** **Apply the basecoat.** Paint 1-2 coats of Newport blue on the sign behind the letters. Basecoat the sky with white painted to the right of the lighthouse. Paint yellow everywhere else and blend into the white. Use these colors to lightly paint the sea as well. Mix 2 parts white with 1 part tattersol brown. Paint this mix on the bottom two-thirds of the shell. Paint the top third tattersol brown and blend back and forth in a sweeping motion until well blended. When dry, repeat on both shells.

Basecoat the sail and the lighthouse white. Use the light tattersol tone for the path. Mix 2 parts yellow and 1 part Newport blue to paint the grass light green. Paint the rocks and chimneys with a mix of 2 parts white and 1 part wooden oar. Mix 1 part Newport blue, 1 part wooden oar, and 3 parts white for the house. Paint the roof, lighthouse door, and shutters tomahawk. Paint the boat and house door tan. Paint the windows yellow. When dry, repeat.

**Paint the sky.**

**11** **Paint the sky.** Mix 1 part red to 2 parts yellow for a light orange, and also make a mixture of 1 part red to 1 part Newport blue for a dark purple-red. Paint a spot of white on the horizon to the left of the boat. Surround this with a swath of yellow. Add another layer of light orange mix, and then a little purple mix in the outer edges as shown. Blend well with a flat bristle brush. Be sure to carry the sky colors through the lighthouse tower window at the top. With a ¾" (19mm) synthetic flat brush, add some clouds by pulling and tapping the purple tone in horizontal taps and strokes.

**12** **Paint the lighthouse.** Paint the cap roof on the lighthouse black. Add some sky tones to the water at the lower right. Blend. Paint a glow in the windows of the house and lighthouse by blending white, yellow, and a mix of yellow and a touch of tomahawk. Paint the left side of the lighthouse a mix of 1 part white and 1 part wooden oar. Paint the rest of the lighthouse white and blend. Shade the white sail in the same way.

**13** **Paint the house.** Paint the house with the mix used before and blend some white on the center of the wall. Add a little black to the house paint and blend some under the roof. Also use this color to tap in the shingles with a ¼" (6mm) flat brush. Paint the door tan and add white in the center and blend. Paint the top of the lighthouse black as shown. Highlight roof and tower with white and blend.

**Paint the trees.**

**14** **Paint the trees.** The trees in the background are painted in first with Essex green, and highlighted with a mix of 3 parts yellow, 1 part Essex, and 1 part white. Use the same colors for all grass as well. Blend as shown. Paint the trees and grass on the land to the right of the boat as well as the trees on the lighthouse and house in the same way.

**15** **Paint the rocks.** After painting the rocks with a mix of 1 part wooden oar and 1 part white, highlight the tops with white and blend. Next, mix 1 part wooden oar and 1 part black and paint on the left sides of the rocks and blend. Highlight the rocks on the land to the right as well.

**16** **Finish the house and lighthouse.** Paint the roof tomahawk, and then blend some yellow on the peak, followed by white, and blend that as well. Now add a mix of 1 part crimson red and 1 part black to the edge of the roof next to the front peak and the lighthouse and blend. Paint the door to the lighthouse with the same colors as the roof. Use some light tan for the trim on the house. Paint the chimneys with shades of wooden oar. Paint the flag with two tones of Newport blue and blend. Paint the fans beside the scene frame a light tattersol. Add the white highlights to the water and the rails on the lighthouse.

**Add finishing touches to the house and lighthouse.**

**The scene is painted.**

**17** **Add detail to the shells.** Add the shell detail by double-loading the flat brush. This is done by dipping one corner in water and the other corner in the tattersol brown. Brush back and forth to blend the two on the brush, and then place on the shell, water side down, and paint a curving line, as shown.

**18** **Paint the letters.** After painting the last coat of Newport blue on the sign, paint the letters ivory with the One Shot sign painter's paint.

**Add detail to the shells.**

# INDOOR CHRISTMAS SIGN

This sign is meant to be an indoor display, carved in basswood and painted with artists' oils, to display on the holidays. It is an advanced project, but with time and patience, is a priceless piece of artwork that will be prized for generations. Draw on the skills mastered in the previous lessons. You will be amazed by what you accomplish!

## MATERIALS & TOOLS

- **(1) Basswood blank, 22" x 18" x 2"
  (559mm x 457mm x 51mm),
  for main sign blank**

- **(1) Basswood blank, 24" x 8" x 2"
  (610mm x 203mm x 51mm), for banner**

- **Chisels of choice**

- **Artists' oil paints: titanium white,
  lamp black, yellow #8, yellow ochre,
  raw sienna, burnt sienna, burnt umber,
  raw umber, French ultramarine blue,
  light red, alizarin crimson, sap green.**

**Christmas sign pattern**
Photocopy at 300%.

**Sign Layout**

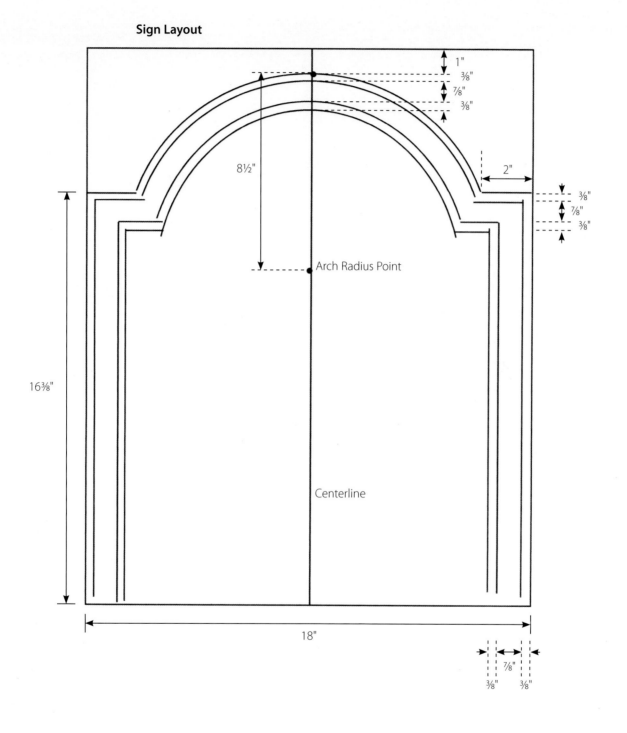

1"
3/8"
7/8"
3/8"

8½"

2"

3/8"
7/8"
3/8"

Arch Radius Point

16⅜"

Centerline

18"

7/8"
3/8"
3/8"

1 **Lay out the design and cut out the blanks.** Mark up the main sign blank using the illustration on page 151. Mark a point down 8½" (216mm) from the top center to serve as the radius point for the arch. Draw the frames and arches. Using the corners cut from the main sign blank, trace the appliqués for the bell, ornaments, and right arm. On the band saw, slice the bell and arm in two pieces on the edges, so there are now two pieces of each one, each about 1" (25mm) thick. Slice the ornaments also, but make one side 1¼" (32mm) thick. This will save some effort in having to carve them lower later.

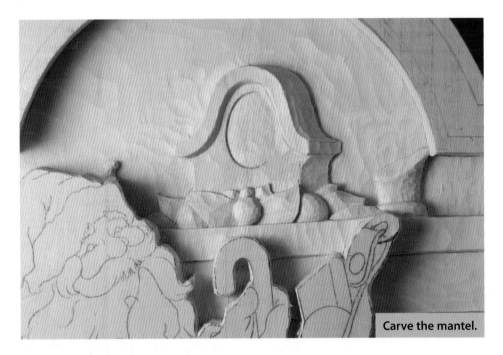

**Carve the mantel.**

2 **Carve the mantel.** At this stage in your carving instruction, there is no need for cluttering up the lesson with notes on which chisel to use—you will know what one to use by now. I will only suggest a chisel now and then. Remember to redraw the patterns as you carve off surfaces. Use the router to lower the wall and the stones on the fireplace down 1" (25mm). Drop the wall an additional ⅜" (10mm) by hand. Draw a line ¼" (6mm) from the bottom on the side of the clock and candles and drop them to this level. Redraw the clock pattern. Drop all the fruit and leaves down ⅝" (16mm). Stop-cut and drop the candle (not holder) ⅛" (3mm). Round the candle and holder. Separate the clock front from its raised cap with a stop cut. Drop the clock face ⅛" (3mm). Pitch the clock's left side lower. Stop-cut and drop the clock face slightly. Drop the "1" leaves ¼" (6mm) down; curve tops down to tuck under. Carve and drop the leaves labeled "2" down ⅛" (3mm). Remember to keep the edges of the leaves sharp, not rounded. Tuck and round the rest of the leaves and fruit in numerical order. Bevel the right side of the clock and cap to give it dimension. Stop-cut around the stones next to the fireplace opening and drop the hearth area ¼" (6mm). Drop the entire mantle area ⅝"–¾" (16mm–19mm). Draw the line separating the mantle from its cap and drop the area below the cap ⅛" (3mm).

3 **Carve the left mitten.** Draw a dotted line where the palm of the hand ends and the wrist begins. Gouge this line and drop the wrist area down ½" (13mm). Stop-cut the cuff of the sleeve where it meets the belly and candy cane. Drop the surface of the cuff down ½" (13mm). Stop-cut to separate the mitten and the cuff. Angle the top edges of the cuff down so it looks like it goes around the mitten. V-cut the line separating the cuff from the mitten and tuck the mitten under this; round the sides of the wrists of the mitten and round the sides of the cuff as well. To lower the palm, make a gouge at the bend in the thumb and stop-cut the candy cane and fingertips to separate them from everything else. Drop the palm ¼" (6mm) and deepen the palm next to the candy cane another ¼" (6mm). With a gouge, put a depression between the two "bumps" of the palm and round all the sides of the palm to give it the final shape. Stop-cut and drop the candy cane ¼" (6mm) and round the sides. Round off the thumb and fingers, and bevel the top of the mitten to make it look like it wraps around the candy cane. V-cut the folds under the thumb and the finger, and then round the edges of the cuts and blend the ends of the cuts into the mitten. Blending the cuts out takes very little effort, but makes the folds look very soft and cloth-like.

Carve the left mitten.

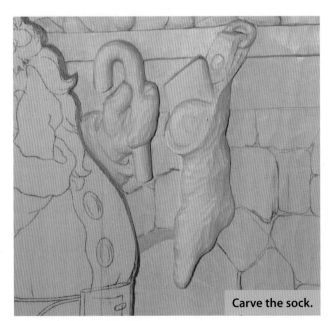
Carve the sock.

4 **Carve the sock.** Be sure to make the surface rounded. The heel and the big wrinkle in the middle should be lowest. Bevel the top edge of the sock back toward the hanger to give the sock dimension and make room for the book and ball inside. V-cut under the ring and loop to make them appear really rounded. Drop and then bevel the book in the sock to give it dimension. Lastly, round the ball.

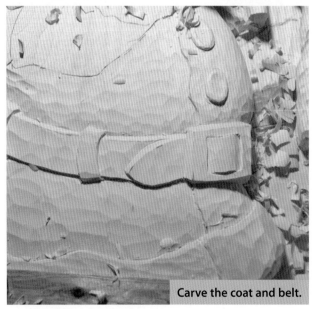
Carve the coat and belt.

5 **Carve the coat and belt.** The belt and fur trim should be about ⅛" (3mm) higher than the rest of the coat. The coat should look tucked into the belt and fur. Round the sides of the coat. Don't hesitate to remove enough wood to really get it round—be sure to feel the carving as you round—you should not feel any square angles. The buttons should stand above the surface slightly. The stomach should stick out and be nice and rounded. Remember that every piece of a realistic carving has levels and angles—for example, the surface of the belt isn't flat, but bevels in around the belly.

**6 Carve the arm applique.** Stop-cut the fur edge and drop the surface of the arm ½" (13mm). Round the sides of the arm. Carve the folds. Stop-cut the edge of the cuff from the mitten and drop the mitten ¼" (6mm) from the top. Drop the thumb ⅜" (10mm) further. Scoop out the inside of the cuffs deeper. Place the arm on the carving and mark off only the part that comes in contact with Santa's body. This is the "gluing platform" for the arm. You will not carve this area. The appliqué will be glued to the carving once the beard and body are almost done.

**7 Carve the beard.** Gouge under the mustache, rounding over to the right side slightly. Round over the right side of the beard and redraw the curls. Gouge the lines separating the curls of the beard and then round them over with the edge of the chisel. Draw in the long S-shaped curves down the length of the curls. Carve them and round the edges. Stop-cut the cheeks and drop the hair on the right side down ⅝" (16mm). Glue on the arm, using the same nail method as in Chapter 5 (page 112).

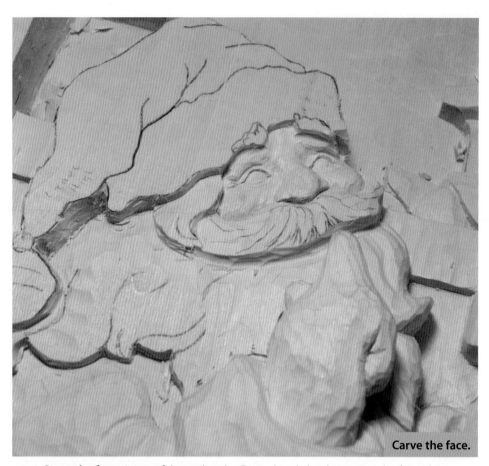

**Carve the face.**

**8 Carve the face.** It is useful to utilize the Dremel and chisels to carve the face. The Dremel is faster than chisels, and has the added advantage of allowing you to focus on the form of the structures of the face without having to switch chisels constantly. The surface of the face can then be carved with a chisel to get the best texture. This method is the best for someone who has never carved a face before. When carving anything, you always begin by getting the rough geometric shape formed, and proceed to refine it, carving more detailed elements as you go. The face carving will follow this process. It is also helpful to break down whatever it is you are carving to its basic geometric shape (or shapes) before you start. In the case of a face, you have an oval or egg shape with a sloped pyramid rising above the surface in the center (the nose). The first step is to lower everything on the face so there is a raised nose. Keep in mind, though, that this face is slightly turned to the right, so the right side must be a little lower than the left. Also, the mustache is a raised element to consider and allow for. The eye sockets are also a bit lower. They are scooped out and then the eyes are redrawn. Stop-cut the eyeball and round it slightly inside the lids—it should have a football shape. Lastly, fit the lids to the eyeball shape—they should only be about 1⁄16" (2mm) above the eyeball surface. Whenever I am carving a face, and it just doesn't look right, I assume the expression of the carving with my own face. The way I have to distort my face to mimic the carving gives me a hint as to where to remove some wood on the carving. It's best to do this by yourself—you may look a little bizarre!

**9** **Carve the hat.** V-cut the hat and bell to leave them high. Round and bevel the beard, hair, and left side of the hat's fur trim down to the stop cuts, at least ½" (13mm) deep. They should look as though they tuck under the bell and folded hat top. V-cut the lock of hair to separate it from the hat brim and round the lock under the brim. Draw on the hair details, using elongated *S* shapes— this will give the hair a nice gentle curl. After carving the hair levels, stop-cut the top of the hat above the fur trim. Drop and round the top of the hat. Stop-cut the tops of the eyebrows and drop the fur trim about ⅟₁₆" (2mm). Round over the trim toward the right. Tuck the trim under the hat. Round the bottoms of the eyebrows as well. Round the top of the hat that folds over the beard. Separate the tip of the hat from the bell with a stop cut.

**Carve the hat and hair.**

**10** **Undercut the sock.** We must undercut the sock in order to finish the stones on the fireplace. Using the #3 14mm fishtail and the #7 8mm fishtail for the more curved parts, cut down and under the sock. Clean the cut with a V-groove, and then a skew, if needed.

**11** **Carve the fireplace.** After stop-cutting all the stones on the fireplace surface, round the edges slightly, just enough to remove the sharp edges. Glue the uncarved bell on and carve it round when the glue is dry.

**12** **Carve the ornaments.** Round the ornament at the top of the sign, first dropping the hanger at the top back ⅜" (10mm). V-cut at the bottom of it to free it from the other two ornaments below. After rounding, remove the excess material behind the ornament from the back. Round over the back of the ornament. Remove the hangers for the lower two ornaments. Drop leaves marked "1" down ⅞" (22mm) from the top. Drop leaves marked "2" down ⅝" (16mm). Round the ornaments, stop-cutting between them to separate. I find using a #3 14mm fishtail upside-down works well. Put a little cyanoacrylate on the tips of the outer two leaves—the grain is weak here, and the glue will strengthen the vessels of the wood cells. Carve the leaves and undercut them.

**13** **Carve the frame.** Draw a line ¼" (6mm) down on both the sides of the frame and lines on the surface of the frame ⅜" (10mm) in from the inside edge. These are the bevel guidelines for the frame. Cut the bevels with a #2 20mm. Glue the ornament appliqués on.

**14** **Carve the banner.** Carve the banner using the techniques you've learned carving them for other projects. When done, trace and carve the letters.

**15** **Paint the sign and banner.** The banner and sign are painted separately and then joined after they are dry. You will be using artists' oils, as you did in Chapter 4 for the Noah's Ark project. These are the colors you will need: titanium white, lamp black, yellow #8, yellow ochre, raw sienna, burnt sienna, burnt umber, raw umber, French ultramarine blue, light red, alizarin crimson, and sap green. Remember to paint up on the edges of the objects that are on top of what you are painting, as we described in previous painting lessons. This makes the edge of things "disappear." Draw on the lessons you've learned painting the other signs, examine the finished photos of the sign, and try to replicate the coloring there. Of course, you can always choose your own color schemes. Don't be afraid to try different color combinations—if you don't like it, all you have to do is wait for it to dry and paint over. When painting, if you can remember a few simple principles, your projects will turn out wonderfully. Always begin with a light or medium tone, add some highlights, blend, and then add your shadows. You will be pleased with the results!

The belt, mantel, and clock are washed with yellow ochre and highlighted with a light yellow mix made of white with a touch of #8 yellow. (See Figure 1.)

Mix 1 part burnt sienna and 1 part burnt umber for a medium brown. Wash the mantel, belt, and clock areas. Paint burnt umber on the shadow areas shown and blend. (See Figure 2.)

Paint the banner with yellow ochre, light yellow, and burnt sienna. (See Figure 3.)

Paint a spot of white on the wall where the flames would be. Surround this with the light yellow mix and blend. Surround this with some yellow ochre and blend. Darken the rest of the back wall with burnt sienna. Paint white on the candle where shown, and yellow ochre where shown and blend. Paint on the wick as well. (See Figure 4.)

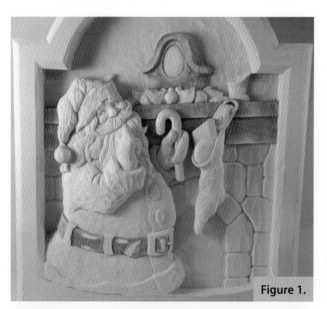
Figure 1.

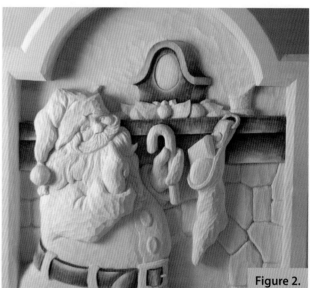
Figure 2.

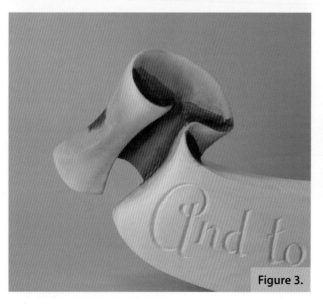
Figure 3.

Figure 4.

Figure 5.

Figure 6.

Figure 7.

Figure 8.

Paint some of the stones raw sienna. Paint the rest a mix of 3 parts raw sienna and 1 part raw umber, and blend them together. Add some raw umber in the upper corner and under the mantle and blend. Add white highlights. (See Figure 5.)

Paint the bell and the buttons with white and light yellow mix. Paint the left side of the bell with a 1-1 mix of #8 yellow and burnt sienna and blend. Paint #8 yellow on the high areas of the coat and hat. Paint light red everywhere else and blend. Add white to the center of the light areas. Paint the hat in the same way, and add a bit of white to the tops of the belt loops and blend. (See Figure 6.)

Go back to the stones and dry brush some white mixed with a very little raw umber. Paint the spaces between the stones on the fireplace with a mix of 2 parts burnt umber and 1 part black, varying the widths of the lines. Begin to add some darker tones to the coat with alizarin crimson. For the last shadow, mix 4 parts alizarin crimson to 1 part black and paint in the deepest spots. (See Figure 7.)

Paint the face by painting the high spots with the light yellow and white mix, and painting the remaining areas with a mix of 2 parts raw sienna and 1 part burnt sienna. Paint the flesh color in the eyes. Add white in the eyes and blend. Mix 3 parts blue to 1 part burnt umber and paint the iris on the eyes. Paint the pupil with black. (See Figure 8.)

Mix 1 part black to 1 part sap green and 1 part yellow for a dark green. Take some of this mix and add 4 parts #8 yellow to 1 part dark green. Paint the dark green in the center part of the leaf and paint the outer edges light green like the leaf at the far left.

The finished bell.

The finished coat, buttons, candy cane, and wall. The sock is nearly complete—just a few more stripes.

The finished ornaments.

The finished clock face and mantel fruit. I used a marker for the Roman numerals and painted the detail in the center with the light green mix.

The finished banner. Mix the paint for the letters using 1 part alizarin crimson and 1 part light red. I used the oil paints to give the letters a softer look. When all parts are dry, glue the banner to the sign. I used some good carpenter's glue and clamped the banner until it was dry.

# INDEX

Note: Page references in **bold** indicate projects.

**ACQUISITION EDITOR**
Peg Couch

**COPY EDITOR**
Paul Hambke

**COVER DESIGNER**
Lindsay Hess

**COVER & PROJECT PHOTOGRAPHER**
Scott Kriner

**EDITOR**
Kerri Landis

**EDITORIAL COORDINATOR**
Heather Stauffer

**LAYOUT DESIGNERS**
Maura Zimmer
Lindsay Hess

**PROOFREADER**
Lynda Jo Runkle

**INDEXER**
Jay Kreider

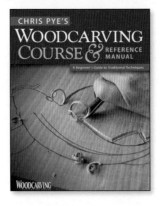
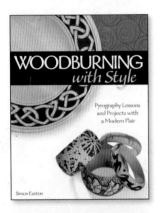
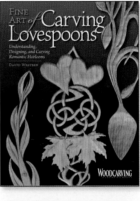

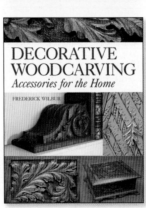